A SLICE OF COUNTRY LIFE 1902-1915

A SLICE OF COUNTRY LIFE
1902-1915

GEORGE F. WALKER

Strawberry Hill Press

Strawberry Hill Press
2594 15th Avenue
San Francisco, California 94127

Manufactured in the United States of America

Edited by Donna L. Osgood

Proofread by Susan Sherman and by Gretchen Stengel

Cover by KU, Fu-sheng

Typeset by Cragmont/ExPress, Oakland, California

Printed by Edwards Brothers Inc., Ann Arbor, Michigan

Library of Congress Cataloging in Publication Data

Walker, George F., 1898-
A slice of country life, 1902-1915

1. Walker, George F., 1898- . 2. Country life—Oregon. 3. Oregon—Social life and customs. 4. Oregon—Biography. I. Title.

F881.W17 1984 979.5'041'0924[B] 83-9279
ISBN 0-89407-037-1 (pbk.)

Contents

LIST OF ILLUSTRATIONS

Acknowledgments

I would like to credit my wife, Lucienne, for her generous assistance and encouragement in motivating me to record some of the incidents and experiences of those early rural years of my life. My brother, Clarence D. Walker of Beaverton, Oregon, greatly assisted with his many contributions of ideas, recollections, materials and verification of the subject matter. I also want to express my appreciation for the interest, suggestions, and pictures of my niece, Clare Walker Tri and her husband Mr. Glen Tri of Hillsboro, Oregon, of Mr. and Mrs. G. N. Tri of Eugene, Oregon, and of Mr. and Mrs. Terry B. Tri of San Diego, California. Mr. and Mrs. F. R. Muck of La Jolla, California and Mrs. and Mrs. F. W. Muck of Sacramento, California contributed many ideas and exhibits. I want especially to mention the interest, contributions and assistance given by Mrs. Doris McKellip and Mrs. Mary Stewart Fletcher of Sheridan, Oregon; Harriet L. Moore, Corvallis, Oregon; Miss Mildred Stafrin and her sister, Ruby, of Dallas, Oregon; Mr. and Mrs. William Stetzner of Butte, Montana; Mr. Cecil Hatley of Pullman, Washington; The Superior Publishing Company of Seattle, Washington; Mr. and Mrs. J. J. Groggan of Walnut Creek, California; Ms. Cathy Baldwin of Willamette Industries, Portland, Oregon; and Robert Nicely of San Rafael, California. My thanks also to the staff of Strawberry Hill Press, and especially to my editor, Donna Osgood, for their efforts and assistance.

To all these people and good friends, and to everyone else who lent a hand with this book, I want to express my sincere appreciation and thanks.

George F. Walker

Preface

More than three quarters of a century has passed since my family left the sod house on the Kansas prairie where I was born in 1898. Our house was austere—the roof had a crop of grass growing on it, and the floor was the good earth, which my mother covered with rag rugs. The fuel for the kitchen stove was dried cow chips, which Mother gathered out on the prairie.

To encourage people to settle in the West, railroad companies put up colorful posters of the good life in Oregon, and newspaper and magazine articles told the same story. My parents heard slogans like, "In God we Trust, in Kansas we Bust," and "Go West—Oregon or Bust!" I don't know whether it was the exaggerated claims, the Kansas winter blizzards, the hot summer dust storms or our luxurious living quarters, but something started my parents' feet itching to go.

In the spring of 1902 the Walkers stepped off the steam train at McMinnville, Oregon. For a time my father worked as a day laborer wherever he could earn a dollar and finally in the autumn of 1902, with little capital, my parents managed to take over a country store and twenty-seven-acre farm at Buell.

Buell can best be described as "out back"—because if you went much further back you would come out the other side. It was seven miles from the nearest town, Sheridan, about a three hour journey by shank's mare, saddle horse, or team and wagon. The roads were dirt or creek gravel, and in winter time, some places the mud would be axle-deep.

The country store was an American institution, serving an important need. It provided a supply point for rural people and contributed to the development of many areas. The country store was a popular meeting place—there was no canned entertainment and people supplied their own amusement. After frequent changes in ownership, the Buell country store was neglected and run down. The previous owners had simply failed to serve the needs of the community.

A SLICE OF COUNTRY LIFE, 1902-1915 will take you to another life, in an important chapter in the history of our country. The customs and conditions of the time in Oregon were typical of rural culture throughout America. I think young people will learn something, and the older group may remember some of their own experiences or those of their parents or relatives.

New Beginnings

The Buell country store was a community hub—for me it was the hub of the universe. The familiar saying, "All roads lead to Dublin" had nothing on our country store. It was located midway on the east-west route from Salem, the state capital, to Tillamook and Lincoln Counties at the Pacific Ocean. In less than a half-mile radius from the country store five roads from Sheridan, Willamina, Red Prairie, Mill Creek and Goose Neck Creek serving the farms, ranches, hopyards and lumbering and logging camps entered this main route. The Grand Ronde Indian Reservation was about twelve miles to the west. For people in the nearby communities the Buell country store was a convenient source for provisions, supplies and conversation.

The twenty-seven acre farm my parents acquired along with the store was on the dilapidated side when we moved in. There was a small house and a barn, houses and pens for hogs and chickens, a root house and a smokehouse. We had a family orchard with a variety of fruit trees, a garden, and fields for pasture and for hay and grain crops.

The water supply was a well about 150 feet from the house. We drew water by rope and bucket and carried it up the hill. There was no flush—this requirement was served by a small building out back with a crescent cut in the door. This facility was usually equipped with last year's Sears Roebuck Company catalogue, often used down to the slick pages of the harness section. On cold winter nights or hot summer days, a person visiting this place would not tarry long.

The store and farm operation had been too much for the previous owners. They had neglected both, and things had fallen into disrepair. They were losing money and ready to move along, which is probably why my parents were able to take it over with very little capital. The fixtures at the store—counters, shelving, scales and such—were barely sufficient to meet the immediate need, with an inventory that amounted to less than fifty dollars. The farm buildings and fences were falling apart, some of the gates and doors hanging lopsided on one hinge.

Because there was almost no money to spend, repairs had to come piecemeal. When we arrived in 1902, I was four and my brother Clarence was two years my senior, both too young to be of much help. Step by step, though, we watched and learned by doing. Before our teens we were assuming increased responsibilities. Everyone cooperated, and soon the store and farm began to show progress. Our parents were hard-working people and patient teachers.

Neither Father nor Mother had any background in operating a retail store, but both had ample farm experience. Father was English and a Baptist. Although he had little schooling, he possessed a practical, well-organized mind. He was a patient, energetic man, admired and respected by the people in the community. One quality that always stood him in good stead was his sense of humor.

Mother was German, and of the Lutheran faith, reared in an all-German community in south central Texas. She attended German schools and was in her teens before she learned to speak English. All her life her English was broken, but no one paid any attention to that. Her friendly, capable attitude quickly made friends. Typically German, she was energetic and ambitious, anxious to make any project she was involved with a success. At the close of a busy day often she was knitting, tatting lace, or making clothes for the family.

Clarence, my older brother, was a born mechanic. His size was far ahead of his years—at fifteen he was a six-footer. I was a light-weight, weighing less than one hundred twenty soaking wet. When we worked together Clarence always took the heavy end and he was in constant demand by neighbors to help them with their work. The going wage was $1.00 to $1.25 for ten hours labor, but that pay scale seldom applied in my case. Whenever an opportunity came our way to garner a few of those hard-to-come-by American dollars we grabbed it.

Clarence had an uncanny ability to repair or construct things we needed. If I wanted a sled in winter, he built it; if a machine or piece of equipment broke down, Clarence usually could make it work. For my part, if I ever had any mechanical talent, it never surfaced—my bent was always along commercial lines.

In Buell, people got the major portion of their living from the land. Almost every family had a garden, an orchard, a flock of chickens, a cow and a few pigs. A family had to be self-sufficient.

Entertainment in the community was mostly supplied by members of the family. In almost every family someone played a harmonica, fiddle, guitar or other instrument, and family sing-alongs around the organ were popular. Nearly everyone had a specialty—singing, recitation, dancing a jig, whistling, bird calls. . . if you had a talent, you were called on to entertain. When families came together and music was the center of interest, usually someone suggested "cutting a rug" and the dance would be under way.

The tempo of life was slower then—people took time to know each other. If a new family moved into the community, soon the neighbors came to extend a word of welcome. Folks were concerned about each other's welfare, ready to lend a hand. How well I recall a time when Mother was quite ill—three neighbor women came, each serving an eight-hour shift for a few days, until she was better. To have offered these women compensation would have been an insult.

Often when folks were at the country store for supplies or mail, they made purchases or picked up mail for their neighbors along their route. If you were in the neighborhood at meal time, you were invited to break bread with the family.

People trusted one another. When they went away their doors were seldom locked—we never had a key for our house. A man's word was his bond—a handshake was the same as a signed contract. If a man said, "I'll pay you on the first of the month," you could plan accordingly. A man's reputation was one of his most valuable possessions, and he took pride in doing an honest day's work for a day's pay. When an individual or a family wanted to buy some special thing, if the funds were not on hand, the purchase would be delayed until the money could be accumulated. Going into debt was frowned on—bankruptcy was a disgrace. The prevailing idea was "Use it up, wear it out—make it do, or do without." The important concern at all times was the family. Everyone worked together toward the same goal, everyone contributed. Senior members of the family were consulted and respected, and cared for in their declining years. The youngsters were taught to do their part. Everyone in the family shared the accomplishments and the disappointments. If everyone pulled together, the family prospered.

The Walker family, 1906.

The Country Store

Starting a new life among strangers with a fifty buck inventory, short on capital and merchandising know-how, but long on ambition and integrity—that was the situation my parents faced in the fall of 1902 when they took over the Buell country store and post office. The floor-to-ceiling shelves and glass cases were practically bare of merchandise, but not bare of dust and fly-specks. It was no wonder there were few customers to keep the store going.

We knew there were plenty of people in the community—people who needed a store there, because it was a half day's journey by horse and wagon to the nearest town. Our only problem was lack of capital. Father got outside jobs working for people in the community to earn a few extra dollars. Mother, with two anxious assistants, took over the job of cleaning the store down to the shine.

Soon the place took on a different appearance. The 28 by 40 foot room and the storeroom behind it were as clean as my mother's German heart could wish. The front porch, with its floor at a convenient height for horse, buggy or wagon passengers, and its roof to keep off the Oregon rain, had a fresh coat of paint. People began coming in just to see what was going on. The word got out: New management at the store.

Often our new customers would ask for things we

could not supply. Father told them we would get the item and have it available at a certain date. In many cases this was acceptable and resulted in a sale, so Father made arrangements with the stores in Sheridan. The merchants were glad to share their profits with him—it was found money for them.

Our parents adopted a rigid policy of fair dealing: Satisfy the customer. This idea spread rapidly in the community and more customers came. Soon the drummers (traveling salesmen) for wholesale firms in Portland heard about the change at Buell. When they were in Sheridan they rented a horse and buggy and made the long trip to the store. Apparently they liked what they saw, and offered their wares on credit. As their shipments were sold, Father remitted payment and more goods were shipped. Soon his credit was established and other firms sent their drummers. The shelves and display cases were filling up.

One day a windfall came our way. A local farmer of substantial means saw our need for capital and offered to loan Father one hundred dollars (a sizeable sum of money at the time) for one year. The interest rate was to be two percent, payable at the end of the year. Father accepted the offer and quit his outside jobs, devoting his time to the store and farm. The money allowed us to take on more goods, and more customers came to barter and buy.

Buell was a farming community, and scattered through the outlying area were ranches, logging and lumbering camps, and hopyards. When it came to provisions and supplies, our country store was the only thing between people and a day-long trip into Sheridan and back. We had to stock nearly everything anyone might need, whether they were farmers, farm wives, lumberjacks, ranchers, trappers, field laborers or travelers.

When the store was fully stocked, a person walking in the front door for the first time might wonder if there was any space left to walk through. Along each wall for about three-quarters of the length of the building we had shelves up to the ceiling with counters in front of them and a space to walk in between. On each counter there was a glass showcase. A back corner of the store was partitioned off to serve as the post office. In the remaining space at the rear of the store there was a heating stove and the bins for bolts, screws and other hardware, as well as brooms, mops, and garden and other tools. Near the stove at the end of the counter were several nail kegs with various sizes of nails. Folks waiting for their mail often sat on these nail kegs.

The shelves on one side of the store were stocked with provisions. Things like sugar, coffee, tea, oatmeal, rice beans, crackers and dried fruit were sold in bulk, and had to be weighed and packaged for each customer. Our scales, wrapping paper and twine were handy. Sugar sold for fourteen pounds to the dollar, and coffee for twenty cents a pound. We had no way of keeping fresh meat, so we sold only smoked, salted or canned meats. We had a

The Buell Country Store, 1911.

broad offering of canned vegetables, fruits and seafood as well. The glass cases on this side held an assortment of candies and at the far end of the counter was a case for a big wheel of Tillamook cheese.

The shelves on the other side of the store held the dry goods, men's work clothes, underwear, shoes and rain gear. A pair of bib overalls cost seventy-five cents, a cambric shirt thirty cents, and a pair of leather work shoes three dollars. We sold women's wear (my mother waited on the modest female customers when it came to clothing), bolts of calico, gingham, cheese cloth, oilcloth and toweling. In the glass cases were sewing and knitting materials.

We stocked a complete line of patent medicines for humans and animals. A visit from a doctor or vet meant many hours travel for the medical man and a fee of three dollars. For people we sold Peruna, Swamp Root, sarsaparilla and Scott's Emulsion for building up the blood, Arnica Salve for open wounds, Sloan's Liniment for rheumatism and aches, castor oil, Cascara and Epsom Salts for laxatives, Lydia Pinkham's Vegetable Compound for Women and Castoria for the babies, as well as quinine, turpentine, Spirits of Niter, camphor, Carter's Little Liver Pills, Doan's Kidney Pills and various ointments.

For the livestock, we had a wide assortment of veterinary medical supplies manufactured by a company in Chicago. The company supplied a catalogue to dealers with instructions for using their products for each breed of farm animal and poultry. It was illustrated with color pictures, and whenever I got a chance I had my nose in this big book, thumbing through it so many times it was dog-eared. When folks at the country store talked livestock or poultry, I had donkey ears.

We sold livestock liniment for swelling of hock or leg joints, sprains and bruises. For cuts and open wounds there were turpentine, iodine and laudanum. We had bag balm for dairy cattle—when a cow's teats cracked, or milk caked in the udder, bag balm was the remedy. It was also good for healing the castration incisions when we neutered colts, calves and pigs. Constipated animals got a drenching of Epsom Salts or Crotin Oil down the throat.

We were glad to have these remedies handy when an emergency developed on our farm or our neighbors'. Once, when one of our horses got tangled in a barbed-wire fence and cut a front leg, my father used turpentine to disinfect the wound. He sent me running to the store for the laudanum, explaining that it would help seal the cut. In a couple of weeks the wound had nearly healed and the horse could work again.

Suspended from the store ceiling were pots, kettles, buckets, lanterns, buggy whips, and from time to time a bunch of bananas, which cost five cents for two. We had rock salt for preserving meats, and cake salt for livestock. There was coal oil for lamps and lanterns, linseed oil for paints, neatsfoot oil for preserving harnesses and waterproofing shoes, machine oil for farm machinery and axle grease for wagons and buggies. In the storeroom at the back we kept 50-gallon barrels for coal oil and vinegar. Customers brought their own containers and we served them from the barrels. We also had cases of soda-water and sacks of salt and flour back there. We had chicken house spray to eliminate lice and Blue Vitriol to prevent grain smut. Every available space on shelves, under counters and on the floor was used. Father's policy was to have what people wanted. If they didn't see it, they could ask for it. We usually had the item.

The store operated at the convenience of the customer. There were no store hours posted at the door. Often, while we were eating a meal, a shout would come from the store and Father left his meal to wait on the customer. This sometimes happened on Sunday morning, while Father was using his straight-edge razor. Without wiping the soap off his face, he would go out to the store. When I asked why he went out with lather on half his face, he explained that it encouraged the customer to finish his business quickly and be on his way, instead of stopping for a chat. It was here I learned my first lesson in dealing with people.

Barter was an accepted way of doing business at our country store—it had to be, since a farmer or rancher had cash only a few times a year, when crops were marketed or livestock sold. We took in eggs, butter, poultry, livestock, fur pelts, Chittem bark, Indian baskets, and other items in exchange for provisions and supplies.

Eggs were a favorite barter item. In the spring and summer many farms and ranches would have a surplus. Often, eggs were considered pin money for the housewife—probably about the only cash she ever saw for personal items. We sold the eggs to logging or lumbering camps or shipped them in crates to wholesale houses in Portland.

Eggs could be a problem. Nobody, but nobody wants to buy eggs that aren't fresh. Occasionally a hen would steal out her nest away from the hen house. If and when the eggs were found, some of them may have been around too long and might be a bit over-ripe. If any of the bad ones got mixed with the others and they arrived at the country store...well, we could not afford to doubt the farmer, but we certainly did not want to sell them to a buyer. If the egg shell had a shine or a slick look, we would give it a shake, and if there was movement inside the egg, it was set aside and buried later. If you are ever so unlucky as to break one of these eggs, there will be a stink you will never forget.

Butter was another common barter item. In the summer, we kept butter in the well, our only cool spot, suspended in a bucket just above the water. Some women in the neighborhood were known for their excellent butter, and their production was always in demand. A few, however, in churning the cream, failed to work all the buttermilk out of the butter. Soon it would turn rancid and the butter had to be fed to the pigs. We were well aware of the situation, but Father did not want to insult any of the women regarding their butter-making abilities, so he cheerfully took in all the butter that was brought to him. Since we had a farm as well as the store, we could take in poultry and livestock for barter. A customer might bring in a coop of chickens, a calf or a pig or two to barter for provisions. Once, a farmer brought a Jersey cow. I inherited the job of milking the cow, and the day we got rid of her was a red letter day for me. Chickens, calves and pigs could be sold to a slaughterhouse in Sheridan, or the pigs could be fattened and converted into cured meat to sell at the store or to the logging and lumber camps.

During winter men often brought fur pelts to the store. Father would pay twenty-five cents for a civet cat, fifty cents for skunk or coon, seventy-five cents for fox and two dollars for mink, martin or fisher. Sometimes the pelts were not dry enough to ship, so we tacked them to the back wall of the woodshed to dry out. If they were skunk skins, it was one smelly place. I avoided going near it. When the pelts were dry Clarence and I baled and wrapped them, and Father shipped them to a buyer in St. Louis.

Also in winter, when farm work was slack, men would earn a little extra money with Chittem bark. The bark was peeled about three-quarters of the way around the branch or trunk of the tree, leaving a strip of bark so that the tree would not die and another crop would grow. When the bark was dry they brought it to the store. We shipped it to a drug company in Portland where it was made into a laxative product. We carried laxatives among our patent medicines at the store, but the natives seldom bought them—they chewed Chittem bark. Satisfactory results always assured.

Folks would bring us their scrap metal—a copper kettle that leaked, the copper bottom from a lantern, an old wash boiler—and Father paid for it by the pound. Twice a year the junkman came through the neighborhood with his cry of "Any rags, any bottles, any bones today?" Father sold the scrap metal to him, and he hauled it away in his beaten-up old junk wagon.

Whenever a barter deal was completed, if it wasn't an even exchange, Father recorded the difference on a strip of cardboard from an empty shirt box, cut to fit in the cash drawer. This way, Father could keep a running tally of how much each customer owed him, or how much he owed them.

The post office was an important part of the store operation. We sold stamps, registered letters, wrote money orders, cancelled stamps, dispatched the mail at eight and received mail at four, six days a week. Father's only compensation was the value of the stamps cancelled, one cent for postcards and two cents for letters. It came to about twenty-four dollars a year.

Folks would come early and wait for their mail, glad of the chance to chat with their neighbors. Tall tales circulated, growing bigger and bigger with each telling. Many wild animals were killed, big fish caught, acres of land plowed, tons of hay baled, Democrats or Republicans elected or defeated, all while the assemblage was sitting on nail kegs around the wood-fired stove waiting for the mail. The country store became a community meeting place. Sooner or later, everyone came to the store.

The store also had one of the few telephones in the area. The line came from Dallas, twelve miles away. There were several phones on the line—the "party line." The phone was a hand-cranked job powered by dry cell batteries. The country store "call" was two long rings, one short ring and another long ring. Whenever our call rang, a series of clicks sounded on the line. We knew that the "party line" was operating.

We saw all kinds of people at the store—just being there was an education for Clarence and me. The Grand Ronde Indian Reservation was about ten miles to the west. The Indians traveled back and forth with teams and wagons to the central Willamette Valley to work in the fields, orchards and hopyards, and stopped over at the Buell campground. The squaws brought willow baskets to the store to trade for provisions and supplies. The baskets ranged from small trays to marketing baskets to large clothes-washing baskets. They served a wide range of household and farm uses, and there was a constant demand for Indian baskets at the store.

The Indians used a jargon language that some of the local people could talk and understand. If an Indian did not understand, he would say, "No cume tux." If they did not believe what they were being told, they would reply, "Hi u clata wah," meaning "You better go your way." Through signs, perseverance, and patience, finally an understanding would be reached. My father was always careful not to strike too hard a bargain, and he soon gained the confidence of the Indians. We always had a good supply of baskets.

On their trips back to the reservation, often the old squaws drove the team. The squaws of a certain vintage had three faded-out blue-green stripes tattooed on their chins. We referred to these squaws as "one hundred-elevens." It was some special designation or recognition used by the tribes.

Each year a caravan of gypsies traveled through Buell, and stopped at the public campground for a few days. The gypsy men always had some extra horses to sell or trade. They were shrewd traders and knew all the ways to doctor a horse. In a few days, after the caravan had moved on, the horse frequently turned out to be nothing but a nag. The local almost always came out second best.

The gypsy women, dressed in flowing, colorful blouses and skirts, would engage in the art of fortune-telling. Usually the act started with "Put a dollar in my hand, it will bring you good fortune. I tell you all about it—put a dollar in my hand." It was all very convincing and often the person handed over the dollar to learn about his or her fortune. That was the end of the dollar.

The gypsies were exciting and mysterious, and provided a topic of conversation long after their wagons had disappeared from the Buell campground. They lived by their wits, often at the expense of the local people, and when they came into the store we were all on the job to keep them from getting back of the store counters. On the whole the gypsies were an unwelcome group and we were glad when they were on their way.

At that time, freight was hauled by team and wagon from the central Willamette Valley to the Pacific coast. The freight haulers usually stopped at the country store, either headed west with their dry goods and provisions, or on the return trip with Tillamook cheese or with salmon packed in sword ferns, which they sold along their route. They sometimes arrived late at night, and would call from the store porch, giving their names, which Father recognized. He lit a lantern and opened the store to serve them. They asked Father if he could put up the horses or mules in the barn, and if they could get some supper. He would say, "I can take care of the horses, but you will have to ask the missus if she can give you supper."

It seemed to me this always happened in the evening after we'd had our supper and the kitchen fire had gone out. I raced to the house to alert Mother, and soon there would be the man at the door. Mother agreed and again started the fire in the kitchen stove to cook another supper. The men would drive the teams to the barn, care for their horses, then wait in the store. When supper was ready, I was the messenger. By the time they finished supper it was late, and after a little conversation they retired to our spare bedroom. Mother still faced the dishes, pots and pans. Clarence and I would lend a hand.

The men wanted to be on their way by seven at the latest, and Mother was up at five to get them a big breakfast. Immediately after breakfast the men hitched up their teams and drove to the store, to take on any supplies they needed for the rest of the trip, and settle up. They paid my father fifty cents for each horse or mule that had been stalled, then asked about the charges for the meals and room. Again, my father would say, "You'll have to see the missus for that part." Mother would be working in the kitchen when the knock came on the front door. The man inquired of Mother what he owed her for her services, and her usual response was, "Let's see, there was the supper, the bed and the breakfast for each of you. Do you think seventy-five cents for each of you would be too much?" The man paid her and she returned to her daily routine. Soon the freighters were on their way.

When Clarence and I were not in school or working on the farm, we would help out at the store. There was plenty to do. Much of the merchandise we sold was shipped in wooden boxes, crates, kegs or barrels, and we got coffee, peanuts, rice, beans and other foods in large burlap bags. Coal oil came in fifty-gallon steel drums, and linseed oil and vinegar in fifty-gallon wood barrels. All these boxes, barrels and bags had to be moved to the storeroom at the rear of the store, and because I was a light-weight, Clarence and Father usually took this job. I got into the act when it came to opening the boxes and crates. The job had to be done carefully to avoid splitting the boards or bending the nails, because they were saved for future use.

After we opened the boxes, and marked the cost and sale price on many of the items, we put them on the shelves, counters, or in the glass cases. These cases usually were in need of soap, water and elbow grease, all provided by the younger Walker generation.

Since many provisions didn't come in their own packages, we wrapped sugar, flour, coffee, rice, beans, and many other items as we sold them to the customer. I developed a "double speed" method of packaging, wrapping, tying and cutting the twine from the package. Whenever possible I pulled this stunt—it was an attention-getter.

Another chore that came my way was roasting coffee and peanuts in our kitchen oven. It was my assignment to fire the stove—don't get it too hot or the coffee or peanuts will be ruined. I taste-tested a lot of the peanuts, disposing of the shells in the firebox of the stove before Mother came around to check up.

One day my job at the country store put me in the way of a real adventure. Early in the summer of 1910, a doctor had come from Dallas to see one of the neighbors who was down with pneumonia. He arrived in the first automobile to be seen at Buell. His horseless carriage was a Pierce-Arrow, a sensation. The folks waiting at the store really looked it over, and I developed a terrific yen for a ride. When the doctor was ready to leave he stopped back by the store and I buttonholed him for a ride. To my amazement his response was "Get aboard the seat on the left side." He got no static from me. The doctor cranked up the engine, then climbed in on the right side, released the hand brake, gave a honk on the black rubber bulb horn, and shifted into low. Soon we were moving, going about three miles per hour, then he shifted into second and on into high gear. . . now we were traveling at the terrific speed of ten miles per hour . . . the dust was fogging up behind us and the fence posts on each side of the road were flying past. Sitting on that soft cushion beside the doctor in his white duster coat, I was in business. But it all ended too soon. About a mile up the way the doctor stopped and let me off. I ran all the way home. No one, but no one in the neighborhood had ridden in an automobile. Folks coming to the country store got an earful about the Pierce-Arrow.

There were other, smaller rewards for helping out around our place. One August afternoon I found myself in the orchard on the business end of a hoe handle chopping weeds around the young trees, with the sun pouring it on at near one hundred degrees. Father appeared on the scene, complimented me on the job I was doing, and said, "When you finish the row, come into the store." When I arrived he asked, "Would you like a cold sody?" The thought flashed through my mind, "Can a duck swim?"

We sold sody, or soda pop, in strawberry, raspberry, cherry, lemon, lemon sour, orange, banana, vanilla, chocolate, creme and sarsaparilla. When the days were especially hot we filled a wood washtub with cool water from the well and kept the bottles in the tub. The bottles were sealed with a rubber seal inside the neck of the bottle. The seal was attached to the end of a metal hook arrangement and when pulled up tight, the rubber sealed the bottle. To open the bottle, you would press down the metal hook, and the carbonated drink foamed and overflowed like champagne, hence the name "soda pop."

It was a common thing for folks at the country store to have a sody, but it was no common thing for me because, after all, a sody cost five cents and required a special occasion. Now that my special occasion had come, my problem was to pick just one flavor out of all those in the tub. This situation required some deep consideration. I looked at each bottle and read the label...it was a tough decision...finally I came to sarsaparilla. I had never tasted it, but it was a favorite among the older folks.

The name sarsaparilla intrigued me and I decided to plunge. Pushing down the rubber seal was tough for me, but I finally managed it. I had to get my mouth over the top of the bottle quickly, because the sody was foaming all over the place. After the first swallow I regretted my choice. . .it tasted like medicine. I did not like it at all, but it was cool, and finally I got about half of it down, then no more. That was my first and last exposure to sarsaparilla.

Sometimes, when folks were away from home at meal time, our wrapping counter was turned into a lunch counter. The customer would select a can of deviled ham, vienna sausage, corned beef or sardines, or maybe a slice of cheese and five cents worth of crackers, and a bottle of soda pop to wash it all down. Father would spread out a clean sheet of wrapping paper on the counter and the customer was left to enjoy his lunch.

The country store became the center of community life in Buell. People gathered there to talk over anything worth talking about—every piece of news, all the neighborhood gossip, every social get-together was brought up in the conversation at the store. Many community projects had their beginnings in the discussions around the stove at the back of the store while folks waited for their mail.

One of these projects was the public weighing scale that we built not far from the store. The farmers' hay and the ranchers' livestock were sold by weight, the nearest public scale was four hours away. Several men in the neighborhood joined with Father to build scales in Buell. One man donated the land, others contributed money or labor, and Father took over the management of the operation. Whenever there was weighing to be done, Mother took over the store, and he would open the scales.

A wagonload of hay or a few cows could be weighed without much trouble, but a herd of range cattle was another matter. They were wild and dangerous, and there was always plenty of action when they came in. Many of the cattle had never seen a man except on a saddle horse, and they had been brought to the scales through new and strange surroundings. The holding yards, pens, gates and weighing platform enclosure were built of heavy planks to a height of eight feet, for very good reason. At the entry gates of the holding pens it required all hands, several men, horses, and dogs, to get them into the enclosure. The cattle were powerful animals and rammed the walls trying to break out. After a group were weighed, they were released out the opposite side of the scales into holding pens, and another group would be brought in. It was an exciting scene—I liked to be around to watch the action, but I always kept plenty of distance between me and wild range cattle.

In stormy weather or slack times between crop planting and harvest, men would come to meet their neighbors at mail time. Their wives came along to visit with Mother at the house. Father did not make the seating too comfortable—they made do with the nail kegs and empty cracker boxes. There were always one or two salty old characters to lend color to the occasion.

One old man, Charley Williams, was a native Oregonian. Whenever the conversation was about travel, and the time and the audience were right, he would pull this one: "You fellows know I'm an old-timer here, but did you know the only time I was ever out of the state of Oregon was when I went to Portland?" This would set them a'thinking.

Oscar Henshaw was an excellent marksman. He could shoot a .22 rifle, then toss the empty shell in the air and shoot the shell. He rode a saddle horse, and when he came to the country store there would be pheasants, grouse, partridge or quail tied behind his saddle. One day he rode up to the store with ten or fifteen quail tied on and his .22 rifle in the scabbard. The usual gang was assembled, and they couldn't resist asking Oscar how he had bagged that many quail. One shot from the .22 and they knew the flight would be on. Oscar said, "I got them with one shot. They were all sitting in a row on the limb of a tree. I shot into the bottom of the limb, split it open, their feet dropped down into the opening, it snapped shut and trapped them." This held the gang for a while.

Among the characters we met at the store was an old bachelor, Joe Davis, who lived in a cabin in the outback country. He had a deformed left foot, and was known as Club Foot Joe. He got where he wanted to go on a pony, and when he arrived he hobbled about with an oak stick.

Club Foot Joe was not on a pension or relief. He made a living by trapping grey-diggers (ground squirrels), a menace to the grain farmers. They paid him twenty cents for each grey-digger tail he brought them from their property. When Joe came to the country store to buy provisions or supplies, he was no Beau Brummel—six months growth of beard, and his clothes seemed to be allergic to soap and water. Several times when the grey-digger trapping was bad, Father grubstaked Joe, and when he could accumulate enough tails, he paid up.

Joe always had a fresh supply of yarns and jokes. His buddies at the country store learned that there was another grey-digger trapper in the Harmony area, about four miles from Buell, and that he turned in a right paw and got twenty cents each. When Joe came to the store, the gang started to razz him that he was in collusion with the other trapper, and that he had promoted a deal to trade paws and tails, so that each of them would make forty cents from each grey-digger. We never knew whether this was true, and Club Foot Joe certainly wasn't telling.

A favorite topic of conversation among the men at the store was tobacco. Many of the men gave considerable thought to their habit, and each felt he had to have his own particular brand. We had a shelf full of tobaccos.

Cigarettes were the "roll your own" type. The smoker carried the "makins"—cigarette paper and tobacco, usually the Bull Durham brand. Rolling a cigarette was a clever maneuver. The smoker had to hold the cigarette paper cupped in one hand, pour the tobacco from the bag with the other, roll the paper around the loose tobacco, then moisten the edge of the paper with his tongue and press it together. The result: a cigarette! Some smokers became so adept that they could perform the entire operation with one hand, assisted only by their front teeth to draw the pucker string on the Bull Durham bag. The trick was always good for some attention at the store.

When the tailor-made cigarette appeared, at first men were reluctant to try it. To promote sales, some of the tobacco companies attached a folded flannelette print of an Oriental rug, about four by six inches. It was a colorful novelty and created quite a sensation—especially with the young swains. They bought the package of cigarettes and gave the rugs to their girlfriends. Soon the gals started collecting them to make a patch-work covering for the pillow on the parlor sofa or some other equally important project. The brands of cigarettes with the Oriental rugs attached were a hot sales item, until the novelty wore off.

We also carried pipes and pipe tobaccos, a few kinds of cigars and chewing tobacco. We stocked Star, Horseshoe, Climax, Day's Work and Piper Heidstick chewing tobaccos. These came in plugs, six marked-off cuts to the plug, ten cents per cut or a whole plug for fifty cents. The tobacco manufacturer attached a tin tag to each cut, and redeemed the tags for merchandise. When we sold this tobacco, we always asked the buyer if he saved the tags. If not, we collected them. Clarence and I got our first shotgun with tobacco tags.

Chewing tobacco was popular with the men, but a trial to the womenfolk. All hotel lobbies, stores and public buildings at the time had the big brass spittoon sitting handy. At the country store we provided a box of ashes. Still, not everybody's aim was accurate. I never had a desire to experiment with chewing tobacco.

Generally the teen-age boys in the community were not adept at rolling the Bull Durham cigarette, and a pipe was entirely too conspicuous. Their secret product for a smoke was "buggy-whip stalk" which was the lower end of a discarded buggy whip. The wood was porous and burned slowly with a lot of smoke. The boys would cut it to about the same length as a cigar, then peel the cover off and light up.

After considerable sales pressure, I decided to give it a try. It was worse than terrible, burned the inside of my mouth and tongue for days. That did me in so far as smoking was concerned—never again for the rest of my life have I smoked anything.

One day a traveling drummer from Selig Brothers of San Francisco, "tailors to men," arrived in a livery stable horse and buggy from Sheridan. He sprang a new idea: sell tailor-made suits by mail! Father listened to his sales pitch, but with all his other responsibilities was reluctant to take this one on. The drummer had done his homework—he had a convincing story and a large, attractive catalogue. The glossy pages were filled with pictures of suits and samples of suit materials. This allowed customers to use the "feel test," he said, and was a key buying influence. According to the drummer it was no problem to sell a man a suit or an overcoat; also, there was no investment on our part, and the commission was twenty-five percent on each sale. My father held out, but the drummer persisted and finally Father agreed to give it a try. The drummer with his hired horse and buggy soon was on his way, and we were in the mail order suit business.

Now, our community was not Fifth Avenue, and the people were not as fussy as city people. The style of dress for most men was blue denim, and for special occasions their "Sunday best" was from the Sears Roebuck catalogue or the department store. The catalogue on the counter attracted considerable attention. People often turned the pages and admired the materials.

Finally, Dale Ridgeway, a local swain who owned a rubber-tire buggy and driving horse, decided to purchase his first tailor-made suit. He was customer number one, and while the instructions were quite complete, including sketches and pictures of men of various shapes and sizes, Father's knowledge was on the short side. He said he would do his best, but could not guarantee complete satisfaction. This was all right with Dale, and Father took his measurements. To fill in the long order pad required considerable doing, checking and rechecking, writing and rewriting, but finally all the spaces appeared to be filled. Dale laid out the twenty-seven bucks on the counter—almost a month's wages—and the order was in the next mail bag going out of the store.

Saturday afternoon about three weeks later, there was Dale Ridgeway's suit in the mail, wrapped in heavy paper, tied with a strong cord. Father phoned Dale's home, but he was in a distant field plowing, so Father left a message with the family. Dale came in that evening to pick up his prized possession.

The next afternoon, the rubber-tire buggy pulled up and Dale got out wearing his new tailored suit. The Sunday gathering of locals made up a fair-sized audience. The rubber-tire buggy was enough to command center stage anytime, but this time Dale in his tailored suit was a sensation. The fitting may not have been the greatest, but Dale had a community exclusive so far as men's suits were concerned, and he was a walking advertisement for tailored suits by mail from the country store.

From its modest beginnings our country store had grown to be a bantam-sized General Department Store. The store filled a real need in the community, and with hard work and fair dealing, we prospered.

The Farm

Ben Franklin's advice, "Early to bed and early to rise makes a man healthy, wealthy and wise" did not exactly apply to Clarence or me, because our prospects on wealthy and wise were limited—but surely we were healthy.

In May, when grammar school ended, it was "vacation" time—but perish the thought, because each morning it was roll out from under the blankets before six, on with the work clothes, and on the way to the barn to start doing the chores. Father usually was there starting the action, planning our work for the day. We took over and he went to the country store to prepare for the day's business. The horses and cows were in their stalls and our first job was for one of us to climb up into the haymow and pitch down hay, while the other filled the mangers or feed boxes.

The next move was to "slop the swine and juice the kine." In case you are unfamiliar with the rural parlance of that era, in English that's "feeding the hogs and milking the cows." The hogs being fattened were fed ground grain, cooked corn, and for the growing pigs and others we fed them surplus milk, vegetable peelings and other items from the kitchen.

When it comes to milking cows, please do not assume that all cows are gentle and docile—that is not quite the story. At the time almost every family had one or more cows, so they would have milk and butter. We always had three or more. The Jersey cow was the popular breed, because the milk had the highest percentage of butterfat—at least six percent. Jerseys are restless, nervous animals. To sit on a three-legged milk stool extracting the milk by hand into a ten-quart milk pail, sometimes half full or more, holding the pail between your knees with the cow stomping back and forth, switching her none-too-clean tail against the side of your face, and not spill the milk requires a bit of dexterity and know-how. Then there's the ever-present hazard—at any moment nature may let go. This is not an unusual situation in the springtime with an abundance of green grass in the pasture. Milking cows never appealed to me as a career with a bright future.

When one of our cows gave birth to a calf or one of the neighbors brought a young calf to the country store to barter, for a few days the calf would get its meals the natural way. Then it would be taken from the cow, placed in a pen and taught to drink milk from a bucket. This system insures that there will be at least some milk for the farmer's family—otherwise it will be meals at all hours for the calf.

Teaching a lively young calf a new method of drinking milk is an experience you will not soon forget. Just in case you might be called on sometime for this responsibility, I will explain the procedure.

Fill a bucket about half full of milk, fresh from the cow, and set it in a safe, accessible place near the calf's pen. Then try to get the calf under your control. Force your forefinger into the calf's mouth. . .hold it there. . . the calf will recognize your finger as something different that the usual source of meals and will start gyrating all over the place, but hang on to the calf and maintain the position of your finger. Then pick up the bucket of milk, hold it so that you can immerse the calf's mouth, and avoid spilling the milk all over yourself and the calf.

After several of these bucket feeding lessons, the calf will finally get the idea and forget about the former method of getting meals. Your problem will be ended for a while, until the next calf comes along. In Clarence's and my case, we had a surplus of bucket calf feeding, because of the calves being taken in as barter at the store.

After the cows were milked and the hungry, meowing cats were fed, we carried the pails of milk into the house, where Mother poured it through a clean cheesecloth into tin pans to store in the buttery for the cream to rise. By that time Mother had breakfast ready.

Breakfast was an important meal for the day. Mother had been up since five-thirty, to fire up the wood-burning kitchen stove and have breakfast ready before six-thirty. This meal usually started with a bowl of mush along with a pitcher of heavy cream—when you poured it on the mush, it came out of the pitcher in a glob or like a blanket. While this first course was being consumed, Mother put a platter of fried potatoes, ham and eggs, a plate of biscuits or muffins and a bowl of milk gravy on the table. There was also a pitcher of whole milk for the two young up-starts and coffee for Father and Mother.

In case you are not informed on the formula for making milk gravy, I will key you in. After the ham has been cooked in the fry pan there usually is a generous supply of grease and if not, it will be added. Stir flour into the grease and cook it until it is a heavy brown paste. Then add milk and cook it until it is a thick gravy to be applied to the potatoes, biscuits or gems, or sometimes a slice or two of homemade bread. All this is a wonderful cure for hunger pangs.

After breakfast the projects for the day began. Father went back to the store to prepare the mail for departure at eight. Customers often called at this early hour before starting their work. Mother completed her household responsibilities to be ready for whatever the day

Our $4.75 Cotton King Plow.

This Cotton King plow is made with new shape boards, adopted after a thorough investigation of the requirements of a plow for the blacklands of Texas and the south.

No. 18120. 7 inch cut, weight 54 lbs., wood beam.. **$4.75**
Steel beam, weight 73 lbs.......................... **6.25**
No. 18121. 8 inch cut, weight 62 lbs., wood beam.. **5.50**
Steel beam, weight 80 lbs.......................... **7.15**
No. 18122. 9 inch cut, weight 79 lbs., wood beam.. **6.25**
Steel beam, weight 94 lbs.......................... **8.00**
No. 18123. 10 inch cut, weight 82 lbs., wood beam, **$7.15.** Steel beam, weight 97 lbs............... **$9.54**
No. 18124. 12 inch cut, wood beam, weight 100 lbs., **$9.52.** Steel beam, weight 110 lbs. **$11.75**

Our $9.75 Walking Plow.

We believe we offer the best steel beam walking plow on the market. It is a plow that we guarantee to scour in any soil. It is especially adapted to the prairies of Kansas and Nebraska, Minnesota and the Dakotas, but is used in every state.

We illustrate this plow with rolling coulter, but the prices quoted are without coulter. We will furnish 18 inch rolling cast coulters at $2.00 extra when desired. This plow is made with a very heavy solid steel point and extra wide shares, warranted to scour in any soil—to scour where all others fail. Remember we guarantee to use a one-half inch wider share than any other manufacturer.

These are our double board plows, made from a solid wedge-shaped piece of steel which is as thick again at the front or wearing side as it is at the rear, extending with a true taper throughout in thickness to the wing of the moldboards. This is by far the most durable and economical method. The plow will wear just twice as long, and the moldboard can be tempered more uniformly throughout.

No. 18125. 12-inch plow, weight 90 lbs.......... **$ 9.75**
No. 18126. 14-inch plow, weight 100 lbs........ **9.95**
No. 18127. 16-inch plow, weight 110 lbs......... **12.50**

Double Moldboard Plow.

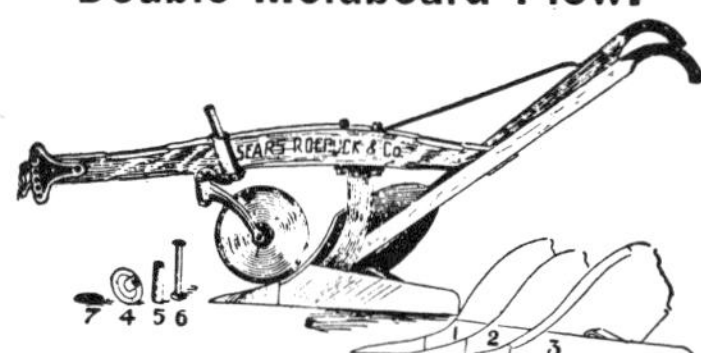

No. 18128. Price for 12-inch Plow................ **$10.00**
No. 18129. Price for 14-inch Plow................ **10.25**
No. 18130. Price for 16-inch Plow **12.75**

We show this Plow with rolling coulter attached, but the prices quoted are for the plow without the rolling coulter, which we will furnish at **$2.00** extra. This is our double moldboard and bent standard plow. The advantages of the bent standard are apparent to any one. We warrant the double moldboard to wear twice as long as the ordinary single shin, or the welded double shin made by other manufacturers. It is well understood by all practical farmers that a patch welded on the shin of a plow is an actual damage to the board. Any farmer that will examine our double moldboard plow will be convinced that it will wear twice as long as any of the other styles. It is the cheapest plow on the market; has a double thickness of steel on the face of the boards. In the illustration we show our new patent cutter and cutter hub. Other cutters attach to the round part of the beam, and so far forward that they do not do good work, and lift the plow out of the ground. Our cutters are attached to the square part of the beam, and nearly over the cutter blade; have a perfect crank adjustment, and made for either wood or steel beam plows. Price of cutter, **$2.00.** Figure No. 1 shows sectional view of plow; Fig. No. 2 shows sectional view of plow, with patched or welded shin; Fig. No. 3 shows sectional view of plow, without double moldboard; Fig. No. 4 shows our cutter hub proper, that can not break, and never wears out; Fig. No. 5 is the hub center, or thimble, that works in the hub; Fig. No. 6 is the steel pin, on which the thimble turns, and if kept well oiled it will last for years. The thimble and pin are the only parts that can wear out, and are cheap and easily replaced. The new hub can be put on any of our old cutters without trouble, as well as on most other kinds in the market.

Our $3.95 Wood Beam Plows.

The above prices are the net cash with order prices for these plows delivered on board the cars at Alton. Ill., from which point you must pay the freight. The prices quoted are net cash. There is no discount to any one under any circumstances. These plows are designed to scour in all kinds of soil, they are made by a manufacturer whose reputation for the manufacture of strictly high grade plows is second to none, and they are guaranteed in every respect. There is nothing better on the market at any price. Made with curved standard, best land side, bar or slip share as desired, right or left hand, as desired, very finest hardened board.

No. 18131. Single board, 6 inch cut, corn plow, weight, 42 lbs., price..................................... **$3.95**
No. 18132. Single board, 7 inch cut, corn plow, weight, 45 lbs., price..................................... **$4.10**
No. 18133. Single board, 8 inch cut, corn plow, weight, 45 lbs., price..................................... **$5.25**
No. 18134. Single board, 10 inch cut, corn plow, weight, 65 lbs., price..................................... **$6.10**
No. 18135. Single board, 11 inch cut, corn plow, weight, 70 lbs., price..................................... **$6.40**
No. 18136. Single board, 12 inch cut, corn plow, weight, 70 lbs., price..................................... **$6.75**

We invite a close comparison of the above prices with those of any other concern. If you do not conclude we can save you money we will not ask you to place your order in our hands.

Our $7.75 Brush Plow.

We offer the best brush plow made at from $7.95 to $10.40. according to size.

No. 18137. 10-in. with Quincy cutter and iron strap **$7.95**
No. 18138. 11-in. with Quincy cutter and iron strap **$8.50**
No. 18139. 12-in. with Quincy cutter and iron strap **$8.95**
No. 18140. 14-inch with Quincy cutter and iron strap.. **$10.40**

The above illustration engraved from a photograph will give you some idea of the appearance of this, the best brush plow on the market. It comes complete with cutter and iron strap under beam. This plow is intended for new and brushy land, where there are stumps and roots. It is very strong and does its work perfectly in all kinds of land. It is also generally used for a road plow, and as such gives universal satisfaction. Weight, 80, 85, 90 and 100 lbs., according to size.

Our $7.00 Stubble Plows.

We believe these are the best all purpose stubble plows on the market, and we are satisfied our prices are below any competition.

This is a very strong substantial plow with 3-horse clevis, adjustable heavy wrought iron standard with extra hardened land side share and moldboard, mate-

required. Clarence's project might be to plow and harrow a grain or hay field. My contribution would be to help in harnessing the horses, hitching them to plow or harrow, opening and closing gates—or anything I could do to help him get on with the work.

After their work was underway I returned to the barn and with a pitchfork or shovel proceeded to remove the previous night's livestock deposits. I loaded them on a wheelbarrow and wheeled it an appropriate distance back of the barn to dump on the pile already there. The next assignment for me, requiring an equal degree of brain power, was to go to the hog pens and repeat the performance. After finishing these two smelly jobs an abundance of fresh air was in order for me—I was no immediate candidate for a social event.

After the plowing and harrowing was completed in the field, Father walked back and forth across the cultivated soil carrying a burlap sack of seed grain, scattering it over the field. Then Clarence or I would stir the seeds into the soil using a harrow and a team of horses.

About this time in the spring the potatoes in the root house began sprouting and Mother began waging a campaign to plant the garden. This was usually Clarence's next port of call with the team plow and harrow. While he was in the garden I was seated on an empty cracker box in the root house cutting up potatoes, leaving at least two eyes on each cut, to sprout when planted. They were followed by a long list of vegetables, all planted under Mother's careful supervision.

The garden soil was rich—Clarence and I had fertilized it the previous fall from the ample accumulation back of the barn. The plantings responded accordingly. . . so did the weeds. During the spring and early summer, the business end of a hoe handle often found its way into my hands. If the weeds got too large for the hoe we pulled them and dumped them in the pig yard, and they were soon out of sight.

Exercising with a hoe and with the sun beaming down, it did not take long for me to develop a case of hunger pains. About midmorning I wondered if Mother had decided not to ring the dinner bell. Clarence packed a one-dollar Ingersoll watch and knew when to unhitch, water and feed the quadrupeds, then be at the house for dinner. I did not rate an Ingersoll—yet seldom was I tardy at mealtime.

Dinner at noon was the major meal for the day and always included ham or other cuts of pork or occasionally other meats, fried, baked or boiled potatoes, at least three other vegetables and the brown gravy, relishes, butter, jam, biscuits or homemade bread. Dessert could be custard, berry or apple pie—often topped with heavy cream or whipped cream, plus the pitcher of whole milk for the two young Americans, and coffee or tea for our parents. After dinner a brief rest period, and we were back on the job.

Each year in the early spring we planted an acre of field corn for the livestock. It was planted in parallel rows about thirty inches apart so that we could use a horse-drawn cultivator to eliminate weed growth. First we marked the field with a home-made drag-type marker that made four parallel lines in the soil. We would pull it north-south over the loose soil from one side of the field to the other, then east-west. Where the lines crossed the corn seed was planted. When the corn grew a person could look down the rows the same as an orchard of trees.

Through the late spring and early summer my assignment was to hitch Old Nell to the cultivator to hold back weed growth. With the two lines of the harness tied together behind my neck, I guided the cultivator as Old Nell pulled it up and down the rows of corn. We went north-south one day, and east-west the next. It was a daily performance, usually with Old Sol pouring it on in the high 90s. An acre of corn is a heap of cultivating and with those temperatures it produced a volume of sweat before the corn was "knee-high and layed by by the Fourth of July." To say corn is "layed by" means that no more cultivation is needed for this season—the corn is big enough so that the weeds are no longer a problem. When the crop matured we cut it down, tied it in shocks and later hauled it to the barn to feed the livestock.

A farmer has to be resourceful, and solve his own problems, because expert help, like an M.D. or a veterinarian, may be a day's journey away. We learned this early.

To this day I bear the marks of an accident that happened to me. Early one evening Clarence and I were cutting up corn stalks to feed to the cows, using a machine called a cutting box. Inside the cutting box there was a large wheel with two long blades mounted on it. Clarence was turning the crank and I was feeding the corn stalks into the box, when I allowed my right hand to get caught in the rollers. One of the knife blades cut off the first joint of my forefinger.

Clarence stopped turning immediately, and reversed the turn to release my hand from the rollers. When my hand came out, the first joint of my finger was hanging by the skin on the inside. I ran to the house, and Mother immediately applied the turpentine and bandaged my finger back in place. She did not use a splint, and when the finger grew back together it was not straight. This accident happened more than seventy years ago, and I am using the curved forefinger to write this story.

In the late afternoons, my job was to round up the cows and return them to the barn. During the dry summer when we had too many livestock on our pasture, it would get overgrazed. A neighbor who had a pasture he seldom used allowed us to graze our cows there. The pasture had a dense growth of grass, weeds, brush and quite a few trees, as well as a stream for water.

One of the cows was something of an outlaw, who

seldom grazed with the others. When she heard or saw me on Old Nell, she headed off in the opposite direction. We would take after her at top speed through the weeds, brush and trees. I would be riding bareback, hanging on for dear life, when Old Nell would pass under a low hanging branch of a tree and I would be skidded off onto the ground. When the bridle reins hit the ground, Old Nell stopped dead still and would not move until I picked up the reins. Apparently she had been trained sometime in her background. She stood like a statue while I crawled out of the weeds and brush and came to her. Then the problem was mounting—my legs were too short. My only recourse was to find a log, stump, rock or creek bank to get elevated enough to get aboard. Old Nell cooperated one-hundred percent and soon we were on our way.

With the outlaw finally under control, and all of the cows moving in the right direction, it didn't take long to reach the gate. Here Old Nell approached the gate sideways, and when I pulled out the locking pin at the anchor post, she walked sideways to push the gate open. When all the cows had passed through, on the opposite side of the gate she pushed it closed, and when I got the locking pin in the post we were on our way to the barn. Old Nell and I were pals.

When the horses and cows were in their stalls and all the other chores were completed it was supper time. Supper usually followed the noon dinner pattern, with some variations and a smaller volume of food, but plenty to satisfy the appetite.

After supper Father took a tour of the barn area to make a final inspection, while Clarence and I gave Mother an assist. On Father's return he often stopped at the root house and brought a supply of Baldwin, Ortley, Jonathan, Northern Spy or other apples. We always had a variety of apples by exchanging with our neighbors. Father placed the apples on the living room table in a large bowl. The heating stove was stoked with oak and the heat poured out into the room.

This was the time of day when all the family were together—unless there was a call from the porch of the country store and Father went to serve the customer. Otherwise he would be reading, working on records for the post office or the store, or talking about an incident of the day. Mother always had a project, either churning butter, knitting, tatting lace, crocheting, patching our work clothes, or possibly making Clarence or me a pair of drawers from an empty, bleached Prize Peach flour sack. If Clarence or I were not plagued with a school homework assignment, we might be playing checkers, dominoes, Jack Straws, or some other two-party game.

Soon the apple bowl was empty and it was the unheated bedroom for the two young Americans.

Summer for farmers and ranchers was a busy time. Many projects were under way in our community: new buildings, repairs to established buildings, care for crops and livestock. It was during summer that Clarence and I grabbed every available opportunity to work for neighbors, haying, hop suckering, or anything else we could do. For a ten-hour day compensation was one buck to one buck twenty-five. We were glad to get the money, and we learned the value of a dollar the hard way.

Crops planted the previous fall or in the spring were maturing, and soon there were new peas, potatoes, corn and other vegetables. Yellow Transparent apples and Green Gage plums were ripening. Now for a word or two about Green Gage plums—don't make the mistake that I did of eating too many on an empty stomach. If you do you will be going places and I don't mean perhaps. For my problem, Mother grated almost a half of a teaspoon of nutmeg and added an equal amount of sugar to help me get it down. Soon I was back to normal, but never again Green Gages.

For Clarence and me summer was off-with-the-shoes-barefoot season. This had its hazards—stub a toe on a rock or step on a nail sticking up out of a board, and we would get the turpentine treatment and hobble around for a few days.

On Sunday afternoons neighborhood boys came to the country store and we all hiked to the swimming hole in Mill Creek. For swimming the boys wore their birthday suits. When Clarence and I got undressed down to our drawers that Mother had made from bleached-out flour sacks, sometimes the bleach hadn't done its job and the Prize Peach Flour Company got some free advertising. It was here I learned to swim by putting a board under my belly, kicking and splashing and having the time of my life.

When we came out of the water, sometimes we would raid a nearby potato patch, build a fire and have a feast—growing boys are always hungry.

Often on Sunday afternoons there would be a baseball game in Rowell's pasture near the school yard. Our team was composed of an assortment of players, ranging from grown-ups to yours truly, the junior member, assigned to the left outfield. Each player furnished his own glove, and we had uniforms with large block letters, "B.A.C." sewn on the back, indicating that we were the Buell Athletic Club. The uniforms were financed by a local rancher, the investment to be amortized by a collection of twenty-five cents (or whatever you could spare) from each male spectator. Each game was ballyhooed to get out as many customers as possible. Our team challenged other community teams, but we were the only one with uniforms.

Summer passed all too fast—soon it was fall and plenty to do. One annual project was wood cutting, since wood was our only source of heat. There were no trees on our farm, but often a farmer or rancher wanted to clear land for pasture or crops. They were glad to have the trees cut down and removed, and we were glad to have the wood.

There were men who made a living as woodcutters, who would cut and deliver a cord of oak four feet high, four feet wide and eight feet long for four dollars. Our parents did not have that kind of money for stove wood, so the two young Walkers were converted into woodcutters for a few days each fall. It was oak for the heating stoves at the country store and the house, and maple or ash for the kitchen stove, and fir for kindling.

My first assignment was to turn the hand crank of a grindstone and drip water from a tin can onto the stone while Father or Clarence sharpened our axes. Then, on a Monday morning late in August, with axes, a cross-cut saw, a sledge, wedges, a jug of water and a full dinner pail, we were off to the woods. Father went with us the first day to line out the work, and after that, Clarence and I were on our own.

When you chop or saw down a tree and it falls in the wrong place or lodges against another tree you are in deep trouble, so you had better know your business. Always chop the trunk on the side you want the tree to fall, or, if you are using the saw, on the opposite side. When the tree begins to lean, move a safe distance away and give the time-honored yell, "TIMBER!" The "timber" call indicates that you are a knowledgeable woodsman.

When the tree is on the ground your work really begins, cutting off branches, stacking them, bucking up the tree with an axe or crosscut saw into lengths that can be carried and loaded on the wagon, and hauling it to the pile back of the woodshed. Later, men with a steam powered saw come through the community and soon the trees are in twelve- and sixteen-inch lengths. I thought this steam-powered saw was the greatest—otherwise it would be the axe or buck-saw and the saw-buck. When the wood was ricked up in the two wood sheds, almost to the rafters, no more wood cutting for another year.

Another job that came around every fall was the hog

butchering. Pork was our main source of meat, because it could be preserved in salt or smoked, and would keep a long time. We needed pork for our own use, plus a supply to sell at the store, so hog butchering was a big project every year.

About three weeks before the hog judgement day, we started the fattening program. Some of the local families fattened their hogs on garbage or grain, but Father was from the Midwest and wanted meat of the best quality. He would use nothing but cooked corn for fattening hogs.

It was Clarence's and my job to cook the corn in a huge iron kettle near the hog house. We would pour several pails of corn into the kettle, then draw water from the well to fill the kettle. Before our evening chores we would start a fire under the kettle, and add more water after supper, then bank the fire with wood for the night. In the morning the kettle was full of cooked corn, like hominy. We carried the corn in buckets to fifty-gallon barrels in the hog house. Father told us to keep the troughs filled with corn, and the hogs never stopped eating. Father's idea was, the fatter the better, because there was a constant demand at the store for pork and lard.

Clarence and I would cut Vine Maple, a hardwood good for smoking meat, and stack it near the smokehouse. We had to have a lot of wood, since meat smoking was a three-week project.

When everything was in order and the weather was cool enough, Father would set aside a special day and folks would gather to help with the butchering. Everybody seemed to enjoy hog butchering day—it was one more excuse for neighbors to get together. The men came to help Father and their wives came along, bringing their specialties for the noon meal, and extra dishes and utensils. For the women, it was a chance to get out of the daily routine, and a time to exchange recipes and gossip.

After a hog was killed it would be immersed in a scalding vat until the hair was easy to remove. The hair was scraped off and the hog was suspended by its hind legs from a pole eight feet above the ground. The carcass was opened, the liver and heart going into one tub and the entrails into another. This tub was carried to a nearby table, where a man with a sharp knife removed all the fat from the entrails, to be rendered into lard. This man's position was known as "gut scraper." Mr. Lloyd Ridgeway of our neighborhood seemed to have a monopoly on the assignment—he was there every year at our place. I don't know if Lloyd had any competition from the other men for the job, but he had none from me—it was a smelly deal, and one slip of that sharp knife and you were in deep trouble.

When all the hogs were butchered and hanging on the ridge pole for the night, the men brought the tub with the livers and hearts to the house. Each family took a portion home with them, happy to have fresh meat for a few days.

The next day we hauled the hogs from the ridge pole to the table in the smokehouse. Father never delegated the job of cutting up the carcasses—he could always get the most out of a hog. First he took off the feet at the first joint. Some people in our neighborhood made pickled pigs' feet. We never did, which was fine by me. I knew what those feet had been walking in! The next cuts were the hams, shoulders and side meat, which he would put in a large box on a layer of rock salt and saltpeter, then cover it with more of the same. The saltpeter would draw out the moisture and firm up the meat. Smaller cuts went into the 50-gallon barrel of salt brine for curing. Other cuts or trimmings were made into sausage or headcheese, or cooked as fresh meat. We used everything about the hog but its squeal.

We kept an eye on the meat in the box and in the brine barrel, adding more salt as it was absorbed. We could judge the salt content of the brine by tossing in a small potato—if it floated, there was enough salt in the brine. When the meat would not take up any more salt, the large cuts were hung from beams in the smokehouse, and we started a slow-burning wood fire on the ground in the middle of the building. It was Clarence's and my responsibility to keep the fire burning, and any time smoke was not pouring out from under the eaves of the smokehouse we got a yell. The smoking process took about three weeks, and meat preserved this way would keep for a year or more. We always had pork for our table and to sell in the store.

For Clarence and me, there was one more major assignment to perform before winter set in. This job certainly did not require any college degrees or special training in social graces. A job description would read: "Hitch up the team of horses to a large sled with high side-boards. Drive to the manure pile. With pitchforks, load the sled. Drive to the garden, orchard or field. Pitch and scatter the contents of the sled evenly over the soil. Return for another load." We repeated these moves until the manure pile was spread on the soil.

After eight or ten hours on the assignment, Mother would almost disown both of her sons. Apparently she did not appreciate the aroma emanating from our clothes, because the water in the wash boiler was heated and the wash tub was ready when we finished the job. She laid down some definite rules: undress in the woodshed, leave your clothes out there, and when you get scrubbed and dressed, wash out your clothes with soap and the washboard, rinse them and hang them on the clothes line. Manure spreading was one assignment we never hankered for, but each year we were stuck.

For the farmer or rancher, the fall is the end of the spring and summer efforts. The barn and haymow and granary are filled, the roothouse is stocked from the garden and orchard, and the smokehouse and woodshed are full. By the time all this was completed, generally it was Thanksgiving Day, which was appropriately observed in appreciation of the bountiful harvest.

Soon the winter rain and snow arrived. The winter weather restricted outside work, so this was a period when we did our catch-up jobs—repairs to tools, machinery or equipment, cleaning the chaff out of seed grain with a hand-operated fanning mill, patching burlap sacks for the next season's grain production, or any other job that was postponed during the busy season.

For the most part winter was a period for relaxation, reading or social functions—cards, games, house parties or community dances, and the holidays. This was the time of year when the roads were bad, and the mail usually was late—dark was coming on by four o'clock. It seemed that folks used the late mail as an excuse to come early to the store. They rehashed the last year's work and prophesied the coming year's accomplishments. Not all these plans matured, but they provided interesting conversation. The larder, smokehouse and woodshed were full, so why worry?

Soon winter passed, the grass started sprouting, and the new leaves appeared on the trees, and we knew it was time to think about starting the next year's projects.

The Blacksmith

A blacksmith in a farm and ranch community is almost as important as a man's right arm. Horses and mules have to be outfitted with shoes and farm and ranch machinery wears out and needs replacement parts. The blacksmith is the fixer-upper. In our neighborhood it was a full day's trip to the nearest blacksmith. Farmers often suggested to my father that he should establish a shop. Father was aware of the opportunity and the need, but there was one problem—a shortage of money.

Father did some research, checking with a blacksmith in Sheridan to find out how big an investment it would take to start an operation in Buell, then he consulted the same man who had loaned him $100 to get the store started. The man was agreeable, and lent my parents $500 for two years.

Father recruited two neighbors and Clarence and set to work building the shop and house for the blacksmith. The shop had to have space for the forge, bellows, anvil, drills, cooling vats, and cabinets, with room inside to shoe horses or repair equipment. The house would need a yard, garden and a well. Being a young upstart, I was the flunkey. I kept a supply of fresh drinking water for the men, picked up scrap lumber here and there, ran errands, held up ends of beams or boards, and generally tried to stay out of the way. At the close of every day I would find myself at the end of a broom handle demonstrating my skill as a maintenance engineer. It always seemed to me that the official slogan around the place was "Let George do it." When we finally finished the buildings, Mr. Joe Campbell, an experienced blacksmith, brought his equipment and family and set up shop in Buell.

Mr. Campbell placed orders for rod, bar and sheet steel in various sizes, bags of anthracite hard coal, boxes of welding sand, kegs of unfinished horseshoes, and other shop supplies and equipment. It was fortunate that the grammar school term had ended, because when all the equipment and supplies arrived at the freight depot in Sheridan, Clarence and Junior were elected official freight haulers.

For several days we made the three-hour trip to Sheridan each morning. We loaded the equipment, including the anvil and forge, into the wagon. Steel bars, bags of coal and kegs of horseshoes all have a strong gravity pull, and sweat and muscle are involved in moving them. For the next three hours we were enroute home, then we went through the whole process in reverse, unloading the wagon.

While we were freighting, Mr. Campbell was organizing his shop. In a week or so he was open for business. Blacksmithing is rugged work and Joe Campbell was a rugged man. He looked as if he had stepped out of Longfellow's poem *The Village Blacksmith*: "A mighty man is he, with large and sinewy hands; and muscles of his brawny arms are strong as iron bands." Joe Campbell had these qualifications. As far as I was concerned, he was made of iron.

In a rural area a man's reputation is his most valuable asset, and it was not long before Joe had a reputation for doing excellent work. A blacksmith had to be an all-around mechanic, skilled in working with metals. He had to know how to repair equipment and make replacement parts, sharpen tools, shoe horses, and build anything of metal a customer might need. One of Joe's first jobs was to build some of his own equipment. He produced tongs in several sizes for handling hot steel, and cooling vats in different sizes, the largest one big enough to hold a wagon wheel flat on its side.

If I was standing around as an onlooker, often Joe would give me the nod to hold up the end of a steel bar or sheet. He used me as an extra pair of hands, and I enjoyed watching him work. I liked to see the sparks fly when he was welding and watch the steam boil out of the cooling vat when he tempered red hot steel. If he was busy, he often asked me to pump the bellows of the forge to heat iron or steel. If my parents wanted me, they could usually find me in the shop.

Farm equipment always seems to pick the worst possible time to break down, usually in the middle of the harvest, when a crew of men will be standing idle until the machine is fixed. Joe often worked long hours under pressure to replace and repair equipment. Many times I saw Mrs. Campbell or one of his young daughters bringing him his dinner pail in the shop, and he would be back at his forge after supper.

One common job Joe performed was shrinking a steel tire for a buggy or wagon wheel. During the dry season the wood wheel rims, called felloes, would shrink. The steel tire came loose, leaving the wagon useless until it was fixed. Joe would build a circular fire on the ground outside his shop and heat the steel tire until it was red-hot. With one or two assistants, he put the hot tire onto the felloe, and immersed the whole thing in cold water to temper and shrink the steel tire.

To clear land for planting, a farmer pulled tree stumps and hauled logs with steel log chains. Like any other chain, a log chain was only as strong as its weakest link, and when a link broke, work stopped. The farmer had to bring the chain in to the blacksmith shop for repairs. Joe came up with an idea to solve this problem. In his spare time he made up a supply of 'cold shuts," or replacement links, that could be used to make repairs on the job. They were a hit, and there was a steady demand for cold shuts.

Joe's most important job was keeping the community's horses and mules shod. Except for a few steam engines, all power and transportation was provided by the hayburners, and without shoes, the horse's hooves would wear down and be tender, and the horse would be useless.

Joe kept horseshoes in sizes to fit any hoof, from ponies to heavy draft horses. He would take an unfinished shoe and heat it in the forge, then bend the ends down at right angles with hammer and tongs. He installed a three-inch metal cleat, called a "dog", at the crown of the shoe. The length of the bent ends and the cleat would depend on the type of work the horse was to perform—they provided traction on the road for pulling heavy loads.

A horse's hoof grows constantly, like a fingernail, though not as fast. As the hoof grows the shoe will need to be replaced from time to time. When a new shoe is needed, the hoof has to be trimmed level to fit the shoe exactly. Joe accomplished this trimming with a special curved knife blade. To make sure that the hoof was exactly level, he heated the shoe in the forge, then held it against the hoof for an instant. Any uneven surface on the hoof would scorch, and he could trim it away, insuring an exact fit.

To nail on the shoe, Joe bent over, holding the horse's leg between his knees. Sometimes the noise in the blacksmith shop made the animal nervous, and there was always the danger of a kick. Another risk was the possibility of a nature call letting go inside the shop. This was a disaster!

Joe's compensation for all this labor, four horseshoes and thirty-two nails was two dollars. Joe liked to tell the

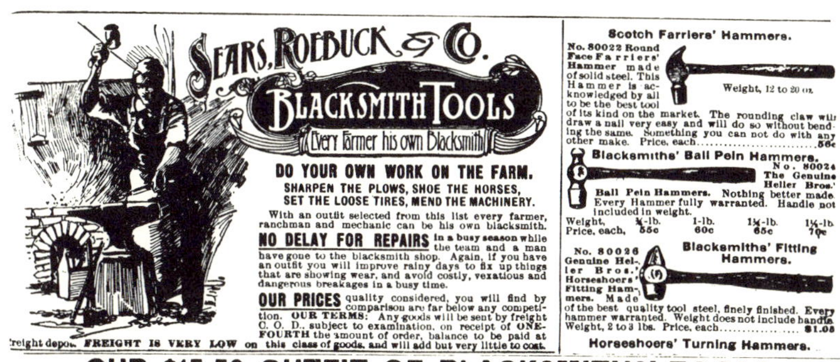

SEARS, ROEBUCK & CO.

BLACKSMITH TOOLS

Every Farmer his own Blacksmith

DO YOUR OWN WORK ON THE FARM.

SHARPEN THE PLOWS, SHOE THE HORSES, SET THE LOOSE TIRES, MEND THE MACHINERY.

With an outfit selected from this list every farmer, ranchman and mechanic can be his own blacksmith.

NO DELAY FOR REPAIRS in a busy season while the team and a man have gone to the blacksmith shop. Again, if you have an outfit you will improve rainy days to fix up things that are showing wear, and avoid costly, vexatious and dangerous breakages in a busy time.

OUR PRICES quality considered, you will find by comparison are far below any competition. **OUR TERMS:** Any goods will be sent by freight C. O. D., subject to examination, on receipt of **ONE-FOURTH** the amount of order, balance to be paid at freight depot. **FREIGHT IS VERY LOW** on this class of goods, and will add but very little to cost.

Scotch Farriers' Hammers.

No. 80022 Round Face Farriers' Hammer made of solid steel. This Hammer is acknowledged by all to be the best tool of its kind on the market. The rounding claw will draw a nail very easy and will do so without bending the same. Something you can not do with any other make. Price, each............ 56c

Weight, 12 to 20 oz.

Blacksmiths' Ball Pein Hammers.

No. 80024 The Genuine Heller Bros.' Ball Pein Hammers. Nothing better made. Every Hammer fully warranted. Handle not included in weight.

Weight,	¾-lb.	1-lb.	1¼-lb.	1½-lb.
Price, each,	55c	60c	65c	70c

Blacksmiths' Fitting Hammers.

No. 80026 Genuine Heller Bros.' Horseshoers' Fitting Hammers. Made of the best quality tool steel, finely finished. Every hammer warranted. Weight does not include handle. Weight, 2 to 3 lbs. Price, each............ $1.05

Horseshoers' Turning Hammers.

OUR $15.50 OUTFIT OF BLACKSMITHS' TOOLS.

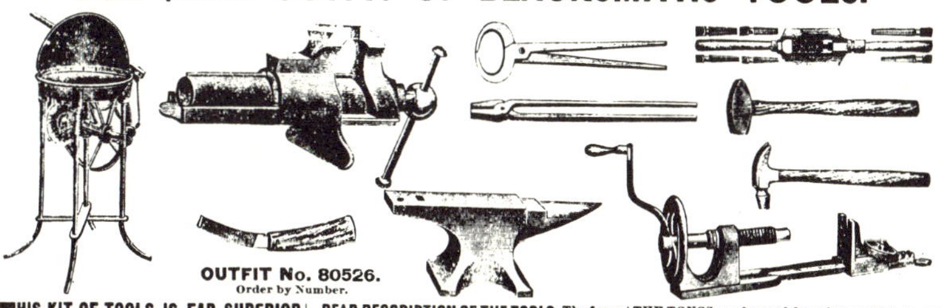

OUTFIT No. 80526.
Order by Number.

THIS KIT OF TOOLS IS FAR SUPERIOR TO THOSE USUALLY SOLD, ALL TOOLS being strictly **First Quality Standard Tools,** such as are used by mechanics. They are not of the class that are MERELY TO SELL. **THE PRICE is $15.50** At this price we ship to any address on receipt of $5.00, the balance and freight charges to be paid by purchaser after examination at the depot. **IF CASH IN FULL IS SENT WITH ORDER $15.50 pays for the outfit,** delivered free on board cars at any freight depot in Chicago. **You take no chances in sending cash in full with order, for we guarantee every article to be exactly as represented** and if not found so the kit may be returned to us and money will be cheerfully refunded without argument.

READ DESCRIPTION OF THE TOOLS. The forge is a lever forge, built especially for farmers' use and light repairing. **The Hearth** is 18 inches in diameter. **Fan,** 6 inches in diameter. **The Ratchet** is perfect and cannot get out of order. **THE DRILL** is a Standard Horizontal drill, screw feed, and is furnished with **chuck to take drills having square shank. THE ANVIL** has a **cast base with steel face and horn,** same as our No. 80478 anvils, and can be used the same as a solid wrought iron anvil. **We guarantee the face of this anvil not to become detached from body of anvil weight, 30 pounds. THE VISE is our Parallel Bench or Farmers' Vise;** has steel face and screw finely finished. A good serviceable vise. Size, jaws, 3 inches; weight, 17¼ pounds. **THE STOCK AND DIES cut ⅝ to 3-16 right hand, 14, 18 and 22 threads to the inch, with 6 taps and 3 sets of dies.**

THE TONGS are dropped forged (no welds), length 20 inches. **THE PINCERS are solid hammered cast steel, length, 14 inches. THE FARRIERS' KNIFE is the celebrated Wostenholm make. THE HAND HAMMER weighs 2 pounds** (without handle). **Solid Cast Steel. THE FARRIERS' HAMMER weighs 10 ounces** (without handle). **All tools are strictly first-class in material and workmanship. YOU WILL SAVE $15.50,** the price of this outfit, in your own time and blacksmith bills. **Shoe your horses, mend your machinery, your wagons. You can do any ordinary work. WORTH FIVE TIMES THE PRICE every year for keeping all your tools in perfect order.**

No. 80526.

OUR PRICE OF $15.50 IS ASTONISHINGLY LOW

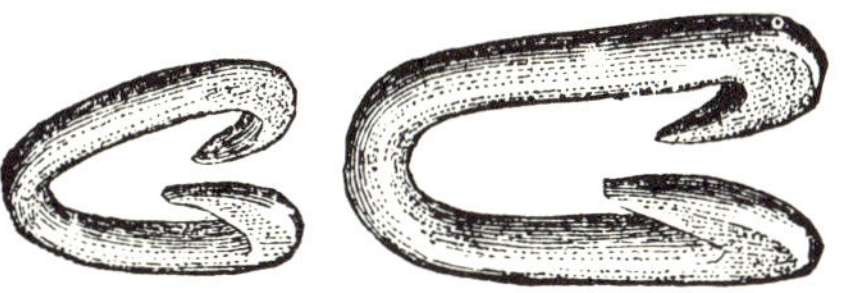

No. 14546. Repair Links for connecting or repairing chains. Size given indicates size of iron from which link is made.

Sizes,	3/16	¼	5/16	⅜
Weight, per doz.,	12 oz.	14 oz.	1 lb. 7 oz.	2½ lbs.
Price, per doz.,	$0.12	.20	.25	.28

For Trace Chains, Halter Chains, etc., see index.

"Cold shuts" — used to repair chains on the job.

story of the fellow who thought two dollars was excessive and that he should get the job done for less. Joe was ready with an answer. He offered to furnish the shoes and the labor, and all the man would pay for was the nails: one cent for the first nail, two cents for the second one, four cents for the third, and so on, doubling the price for each additional nail. The story is an oldie, but if you haven't tried it, get a pencil and paper and figure it out.

Joe operated the shop in all seasons. In the summer, with the temperature in the nineties, standing before the flaming forge was like looking through the gates of Hades and twice as hot. In the winter, handling cold steel with the only heat in the shop coming from that forge—it was rough work. Blacksmithing is one career I appreciated being exposed to, but I never had a yen to be the village blacksmith.

Sheep Shearing

Money was always hard to come by in our store and farm operation, and my parents never had extra cash for Clarence or me. If I wanted something, I knew it was my problem to generate the funds. It was a source of pride for me to have my own money for whatever I wanted or needed.

My opportunities to earn money usually came about at the store. When men came in to buy supplies, they stopped to talk about their plans and their work. I was there to listen, and my idea was "Goods well displayed are half sold." I made sure I was on display. Other boys in the community didn't get such good exposure when it came to landing jobs.

Many ranchers and farmers included sheep in their operations, some with a few head of sheep, others with a large band. A popular saying was "Sheep will pay your taxes." They were good for grazing untillable land and keeping down weed and brush growth, and they did not need much attention, except at lambing time.

Sometimes a ewe would refuse to let her newborn lamb nurse. The farmer would take the lamb into the house and feed it milk from a bottle. In a few days the lamb was stronger and could return to the ewe. There is nothing as cute as a young lamb.

Shearing sheep by hand is a time-consuming workout.

A giant step forward in sheep shearing equipment. I held the responsible position of standing for ten hours a day turning the crank. Drawing by Robert Nicely.

A young man in our neighborhood, Vila Blanchard, saw an opportunity to set himself up as a "custom sheep shearer". He bought a sheep shearing machine and offered his services to farmers and ranchers at a set fee for each sheep sheared. His idea got a warm reception, and he was in business.

The shearing machine was the forerunner of the clippers later used in barber shops. Vila's machine was a hand-cranked model, and that was my oyster. Vila needed someone to turn the cog-wheel, and I hit him up for the job. He was surprised, but he decided to give me a try, and agreed to pay a dollar a day.

The next Monday morning, he picked me up, with the shearing machine in his buckboard buggy, and we were off to the Fogg Riley ranch to start our work. I was equipped with an old tarpaulin, a bed roll made of a worn quilt and some blankets, and a canvas bag for my clothes. We were to eat our meals with the families we worked for and sleep in the barn, or whatever place was available.

Fogg Riley had rounded up his band of sheep in a corral near the shed, and soon Vila had the shearing machine ready for action. He singled out a sheep and grabbed it by a hind leg. There was plenty of kicking and struggling, but Vila was strong and experienced, and soon the sheep was on the floor of the shed, ready to be shorn. Vila gave the signal and I started cranking the cogwheel.

The wheel had to turn at a steady, constant rate to get the proper action from the clippers. If I was turning too fast or too slow, Vila would give me a yell. When he finished a sheep he turned it loose to return to the band, and I helped him gather up the wool from the floor, roll it into a fleece, and tie it in a bundle. Then Vila caught another sheep by a hind leg and we started shearing again.

A sheep's fleece is saturated with an oil called

"lanolin." It smells strongly of sheep, and after handling the fleeces for a little while, we were pretty well oiled up. Neither of us would have received a warm welcome at a social gathering. I wonder if the pretty ladies using facial creams with "lanolin" balyhooed in their advertising know it comes from a sheep's body? They might be shocked.

We sheared until noon, when the dinner bell tolled at the house. Vila finished the sheep he was working on, then we washed up and soon we were at the table. Mrs. Riley was an excellent cook, and the dinner was served family style. I certainly did not intend to insult her by holding back. After dinner we had a short rest, and were back at the sheep shed by 1:00.

As the afternoon wore on, it seemed to me that Vila was slowing down, not grabbing sheep or shearing as fast as in the morning. This puzzled me, because I knew he was paid by the number of sheep he sheared. About four o'clock Mr. Riley came by to see how the work was going. They talked and decided that we could not finish the job that day.

Mr. Riley left and when Vila finished the sheep we were shearing, he stopped for a few minutes. At this point I got some education about working at farms and ranches. Vila had worked all over our neighborhood, and knew his way around. He swore me to secrecy, then told me why he was not working as fast as he had in the morning. He explained that the meals here at the Rileys' were excellent, but at the Starr farm, our next job, they would be lousy. He didn't want to be stuck there overnight, so he decided to slow down here, complete the job after breakfast, then move on to the Starrs' and start there early. We could work fast and be out by mid-afternoon, and we would only have to eat one meal there. This was fine with me, so we started shearing again, and worked until the supper bell rang.

After supper we sat on the porch with Mr. Riley for a

while, then went to the barn to spread some hay for a mattress and make up our beds. We were asleep by 8:30, and up again at 6:00, ready for breakfast at 6:30.

Our stay at the Riley ranch ended all too soon, and at 10:30 we were shearing sheep at the Starr farm, going at top speed. Mr. Starr came by at noon to say that dinner was ready. When we arrived at the house three youngsters met us. It looked as though they had not been exposed to a bar of soap for some time. Later we met Mrs. Starr in the kitchen, and her appearance paralleled her children's. The kitchen was anything but appealing, and Vila had been right about the food. When dishes were passed around the table, neither Vila nor I were very hungry.

We endured the dinner and hurried back to our shearing, then moved on to the Butler farm. At Butler's the conditions were on a par with Riley's, and for the rest of the week we had no more experiences like the Starrs.

When I got home after a week of sheep shearing, my mother got one whiff and decided I was a candidate for the tub. At our house there was an established bath procedure—Clarence rated the first spot, and I was number two. The water had to be drawn from the well and carried to the house, then heated in a washboiler on the kitchen stove. The wood washtub was brought into the kitchen and the water was poured into it for the Saturday night tub scrub. Enter bather number one, Clarence, and when he was finished I inherited the less warm but more cloudy and sudsy water. Generally this was not too bad, but after both of us had worked all week, and especially after my week of wrestling sheep, you can guess that the water got to be pretty thick, and position number one had some advantages.

I admit I felt some discrimination, but I discussed the situation with some of my peers and discovered that the number one and number two bath method was a general practice as far as boys were concerned. Since I had no sisters, I don't know what the system was for girls. I decided I was lucky I didn't have two or three older brothers.

After our second week of shearing, Vila brought me home and handed me a check for fifteen dollars, which Father cashed for me. I felt really prosperous—this was the largest amount of money I had had all at once.

I had never owned a watch, and I decided I wanted one. The latest thing in timepieces was the gunmetal watch, and several men had displayed them to their friends at the store. I developed a real yen for one. Neither Father nor Mother offered any objections, which I interpreted as their strong approval.

On my next trip to Sheridan, I plunked down the fifteen dollars at a jewelry store and walked out with my own gunmetal watch. I got a leather string to use for a chain, and everything was coming up roses. None of my buddies had a gunmetal watch. It was great until, a short time later, I noticed the finish on the back of the watch was wearing down to a different color. This was serious, and it got no better fast. Soon I had a two-tone watch—gunmetal finish around the face, and nickel finish on the back. I stopped parading the watch around and did no more talking about it. I was so low I could have walked under a snake's belly and packed an umbrella. I had suffered an awful lot of sweat, lanolin and sheep ticks for that watch and it was quite a setback. I guess I had learned a lesson: Stick to established brands!

Going to the Circus

Extravaganza! Buffalo Bill! The Big Top! Parade! The colorful posters on the wall of the country store promised all the wonders of the circus. In mid-July of 1910, the advance publicity men from Buffalo Bill's Wild West Show came to Buell to put up the tempting posters and drum up business for the circus. Soon everyone in the neighborhood knew that there would be a parade down Commercial Street in Salem the morning of August 5th, and the Big Top would open for the show that afternoon.

The publicity man gave Father two tickets for letting him put up his posters on the wall of the store. Both Father and Mother had seen a circus, so they gave the tickets to Clarence and me. The time between that day in July and August 5th was the longest stretch I have ever lived.

Not only did I have the pictures with their wild animals, acrobats on galloping horses, trapeze artists and clowns to stir me up, but there was plenty of conversation at the store—Buffalo Bill was the topic of the day. Several of the local pioneer families had come from the Midwest and knew about the accomplishments of William F. Cody, frontiersman and showman. At fifteen he had been a Pony Express rider, and at twenty-three General Sheridan appointed him chief of the Indian Scouts. It was General Sheridan who established the

Grand Ronde Reservation ten miles from Buell, and the town of Sheridan was named for him. Bill Cody was an expert shot with a rifle from the back of a galloping horse. When the railroad was under construction west from Fort Hays, Kansas, he supplied buffalo meat for the construction crew, and this was how he got the name Buffalo Bill. Later he founded the town of Cody in Wyoming. He was a great showman, and this was to be his final tour.

Clarence and I tried to pass the time before the big day planning our trip. We each had bought a new bicycle with money we earned working for neighbors, and we planned to bike the first twelve miles, then take the train from Dallas to Salem. We decided not to wear our Sunday best, since the roads were bound to be dusty. We settled for overalls.

The morning of August 5th finally arrived, and we attacked the chores at five o'clock. By six we were on our bicycles, decked out in our overalls, each with a lunch in his pocket. Between Buell and Dallas were two long, steep hills. Butler Hill was down-grade and, six miles further on, Dunlap Hill was up-grade. Coasting down Butler Hill and pedaling the level six miles went fast, but at the base of Dunlap it was something else. We had to get off our bikes and push them, traveling at a snail's pace up the steep grade. We made a few rest stops on the way up, and Clarence looked at his Ingersoll watch several times—the hands were moving around awfully fast. When we reached the crest of Dunlap, the time to make it to the depot was getting short. Clarence took off at top speed, since he could pedal faster than I could, and left his bicycle at the livery stable where Father stalled our horses when he came to Dallas. Clarence was at the depot when I arrived at the livery stable. I parked my bike and took off on the double for the station. When I arrived Clarence had the tickets and the train was waiting.

I had seen plenty of trains when we were delivering freight to Sheridan, but this was my first chance to ride in one. The huge black engine was an awesome sight, with steam curling out of the steam chest near the steel wheels, and the big gold number 29 on the front. We followed the crowd into the passenger car and soon we were sitting on the luxurious cushions. Clarence, being the keeper of the tickets (rail and circus), rated the window seat, but I was not griping—I was on my way to see Buffalo Bill!

Soon the conductor, pressed and polished in his sharp blue uniform, came out of the depot and shouted, "ALL ABO-O-OARD! If you can't get a board get a rail!" The big brass engine bell started ringing, and steam shot from the engine in a rythmic *shoosh...shoosh...shoosh*. Slowly and smoothly we picked up speed. The bell kept ringing as we pulled out of town. My first train ride!

At every crossing and turn the engineer gave a long blast on the steam whistle. The conductor came down the aisle collecting tickets, talking and laughing with the passengers. The conductor was the personality of the train. There was also a fellow called a "news butcher" who sold the Portland and Salem newspapers, and bags of peanuts, for five cents. The Portland paper was a big deal—when you had read it you were right up to date. The businessmen and farmers bought it to check up on the commodity, livestock and grain prices.

The train was going full steam and so was the conversation among the passengers. Everybody was going to see Buffalo Bill's Circus. Without too much delay Clarence and I let the folks know we had reserved-seat tickets, which did not deflate our stock any. For a while we were center stage, and I aired some of my knowledge about William F. Cody. It wasn't long before we were pulling in at the Salem depot.

We hurried off the train and followed the crowd to Commercial Street. The sidewalks were full of people, craning and stretching their necks to see the parade that was assembling at the end of the street. Clarence and I maneuvered through the crowd to the edge of the curb, where we could see everything.

Buffalo Bill led the parade, mounted on a beautiful white stallion with a silver-studded saddle and bridle. He wore a white Stetson, a white buckskin fringed jacket and trousers, and white riding boots. With his flowing silver hair and goatee, sitting high up on the stallion, he was an impressive sight. An Indian woman rode beside him on a white mare with silver-trimmed saddle and bridle. The woman was also dressed in white buckskin, and she carried a basket filled with glass balls.

As the parade moved down Commercial Street, the Indian woman tossed a glass ball high in the air. Buffalo Bill casually leveled his rifle, fired one shot, and shattered the glass ball. He waved at the cheering crowds and rode on, followed closely by six huge elephants, walking two abreast, draped with fancy cloth trimmed with glistening sequins. I had seen pictures of elephants in school books, but these giant creatures were almost too much. As they lumbered along, one of them came pretty close, and if Clarence had not been there, I might have taken off.

The performing horses followed them, with plumes on their heads and their riders dressed in fancy costumes. Then came the clowns, stopping along the way to entertain the crowds. Next were the painted and gilded wagons with cages of lions, tigers and other wild animals. At the end of the long procession the steam calliope blasted its loud circus music. It had a huge sign on the side,'*The Big Top Opens at 1:30 PM.*"

The parade broke up at the end of Commercial Street, and Clarence and I followed along to the circus grounds, where there was plenty of action. Crews of four men were driving stakes for the Big Top. They worked as a unit, alternating their blows on the steel stake, so precise they sounded like a machine. They worked fast, and soon the ropes were installed and the big tent went up. Another crew hung the trapeze swings at the top of the tent, while others moved the animals' wagons along the walls. Other men set up the bleacher seats and laid out three performance rings in the center of the tent. It was action, action and more action, and Clarence and I watched until the sides of the tent were lowered and cut off our view.

Talking with one of the crewmen, we learned that after the 7:30 show it would all come down again and be loaded on the train to move during the night to the next town.

By this time our stomachs were screaming. We found a shady spot and polished off our lunches. When we got back the sideshow barkers were hawking their offerings—The Fat Lady, The Strong Man, The Three-Legged Calf, Tom Thumb and others. We did not indulge in any of these, since the tickets were fifty cents each and we did not have that kind of dough to squander.

Soon the gate to the Big Top opened. Clarence handed our tickets to the taker, who directed us to an usher. We found ourselves seated in front of the center ring in a choice spot. The crowd poured in and soon all the seats were filled. The calliope blasted out a fanfare as Buffalo Bill and the Indian woman rode in to a big welcome from the crowd. They rode around the edge of the Big Top, and again the woman tossed glass balls into the air, and Buffalo Bill never missed a shot, to the delight of the audience.

Bill Cody was known for his excellent marksmanship, but how could he handle his rifle so casually, riding a galloping horse, and never miss the glass ball? This might not bother the city people, but Clarence and I were familiar with rifles, and we didn't understand how it could be done. Later, we asked some of the men at the store. They told us that the shells were not bullets, but buckshot, which sprays out in a wide pattern. How could he miss? Buffalo Bill was a true showman.

By this time there was action in all quarters, with wild animals in one ring, dancing horses in another, elephants and clowns in the third, and acrobats on the swinging trapeze bars above our heads. We tried not to miss anything, turning our heads from side to side, up and down, but it was too much to take in all at once. The bags of peanuts we had bought melted away before we even noticed.

At last the lights flashed, and Buffalo Bill rode out once more for a final bow. Clarence kept an eye on his watch, and all too soon we had to leave our reserved seats and doubletime it to the depot to catch the 4:30 train back to Dallas. We ran all the way, and when we arrived the train was ready to pull out. Some of the people we had met on the morning train were going aboard. We were a bit on the worn side, and the cushions looked good to us.

Soon the conductor appeared and called "All Aboard!" and we were headed home. The return trip was a re-hash of the events of the day—everyone had a story to tell until we arrived at the Dallas depot at 5:15.

Walking to the livery stable for our bikes, we passed a bakery, and the cinnamon rolls in the window were more than we could resist. We took on a dozen for an investment of twenty-five cents. From the livery stable it was a short distance out of town. We stopped in the shade of a tree and took care of the cinnamon rolls—it was easier to carry them on the inside than on the outside. At the top of Dunlap hill, that long down-grade looked good, coasting for more than a mile. The six miles of level ground weren't too bad, but at the base of Butler Hill . . . well, with only a pocket lunch, a quarter pound of peanuts and a half-dozen cinnamon rolls under my belt, I had had it. We started walking, pushing the bikes up the grade, but I started slowing down. Clarence took over the job of pushing both bicycles up the hill—don't underestimate that problem! Finally we were at the top and the rest of the road was level. By eight o'clock the country store came into view and, let me tell you, it was a welcome sight. It gave me a shot of adrenalin and the bike pedals pumped easier.

Mother had supper ready, and Clarence and I did justice to her meal. We told our story, and soon it was bedtime. For the next several days at the store, the spotlight was on us—we were the only ones from Buell who had been to the circus.

Hunting and Fishing

Hunting and fishing skills were important in our area, since they provided much of the meat on many families' tables. Venison could be served fried, roasted, baked or stewed, or dried for jerkey, and game birds and fish were also welcome. Because there was no way to preserve fresh meat, when a deer was killed the meat would often be shared with the neighbors.

Wild game's first law is self-preservation, and they are experts at it. For example, when a deer knew hound dogs and hunters were on its trail, it would run for a distance, then start to circle, doubling back over and across the trail. Then it would go a short distance and make another circle. If there was a creek in the area, the deer would head for it, wade or swim for some distance, then come out on the other shore. These wily stunts will confuse many dogs—they will lose the trail and the hunt is over.

Some hunters preferred still hunting, with no hound dogs involved. Deer have regular runs to and from their water or feeding grounds. The hunter selects a secluded spot to hide, where he can see the trail in both directions. Here he sits and waits, and when the deer comes into view, he usually gets his venison. Of course, there's always the chance that he will sit for hours and never see a deer.

When the hunter bags his deer, he carries it home or

packs it to a place where he can remove the entrails, to prevent spoilage. The carcass is hung for twelve hours or more to let the body heat dissipate.

Game birds can be masters of deception. You might decide to get a big grouse for the family dinner table. These birds live in tall fir or pine trees in the forest. You are walking along with your gun, and you hear the grouse's hoot. You are now in business—the hoot was some distance away, but you think you can spot the tree where the grouse is hiding. Softly and slowly you walk in the direction of the hoot. . .finally you think you have the right tree and you walk quietly under it. . .but there is no more hooting. All is quiet for a few minutes, then the hoot starts again—from a tree some distance away. You try again, and arrive at the second tree, and again the hoot is behind or beyond you. This bird can outwit you, and almost drive you berserk. The grouse is the world's best ventriloquist.

Another crafty bird is the quail. When a mother quail with a flock of chicks is alarmed, she will give a signal and the chicks disappear. The hen pretends to have a broken wing and struggles away, flopping her wing, squawking loudly. The hunter follows, figuring on easy game. When the chicks are safe, she flies away.

In the late afternoon, when I went to the woods to bring the cows back to the barn, I took my .22 rifle along. If a quail, pheasant or grouse flew out and luck was with me, we would have some fresh meat. When the cows were safely in the barn, my next project was to remove the feathers and the entrails, and hang the bird in a cool place for the night. We never cooked game or fresh meat until it was cooled.

Wild geese were another source of meat in the late fall. Hundreds flew south for the winter, and returned in the early spring. We kept a 12-gauge single-barrel shotgun in the house. One day in November a large flight passed over the house. Father grabbed the 12-gauge and rushed out. He fired one shot into their close formation, and four geese fell to the ground.

Mother wanted the feathers for a comforter. If you have ever slept under a down comforter, you know it is the deluxe of all covers for a bed, lighter and warmer than any other. No matter how careful you are in picking the feathers from the bird, the down gets in the air and floats all over the place. It gets into everything. We forgot about our picking problems, though, as we enjoyed a fresh goose dinner. Mother, being German, knew how to cook a goose.

Trapping fur-bearing animals was a source of income. The trappers brought furs into the store to barter for provisions and supplies. They had to be careful setting the traps—the animals avoided the trap if it had been touched by human hands.

Joe Parker, a rancher who lived about a mile from our place, trapped a big skunk that was raiding his chickens. Talking about it at the store, Joe mentioned that he was not going to bother to skin it. This was my opportunity, and I asked if I could have it, because Father paid fifty cents for a skunk pelt. It was all right with Joe, and I sharpened up my trusty pocket knife and was soon at the Parker ranch. The skinning was no problem, since I had skinned several squirrels. I threw the carcass into a deep canyon, and was on the way home with my prize. I tacked the skin to the back wall of the woodshed to dry.

When I arrived in the kitchen, I found that skunk aroma and Mother were not compatible. Apparently she had been tipped off, because the washboiler was heating on the kitchen stove and the washtub was waiting in the woodshed. She invited me to take off my clothes in the woodshed and leave them there, then get into the tub and scrub myself. She got no comment from me—only action. When I got out of the tub the clothes went into it, and after plenty of scrubbing with a washboard and a bar of soap, they were hung on the clothes line. After this ordeal Mother was much friendlier, and I decided I had had enough of skunk skinning.

Men took a lot of pride in their hunting dogs. Mr. Frank Dickey lived far back in the hill country, and whenever he rode in to the store, his dog Shep was with him. Like other ranchers and farmers, he was always ready with his rifle, and often there was game tied to the back of his saddle. One day he came into the store about noon, and bought a can of corned beef and some crackers for his lunch. Then he turned to me and asked for another can. He opened the second can and put it on the floor in front of Shep. I had never seen such extravagance—a can of corned beef cost twenty-five cents! It certainly indicated Mr. Dickey's high regard for his dog.

In a farming and ranching community, a marauding bear, wolf, cougar or bobcat will kill valuable livestock. The killer has to be eliminated, and the hunt provides plenty of excitement. If you decide to come along, one of the ranchers will equip you with a saddle horse and a long-range rifle. You will join the other men in the neighborhood at dawn near the place where the most recent kill was made. Everyone will be assigned a lookout station, then the dogs are released and the action begins.

The dogs pick up the scent and are on their way, barking and yelping. They are soon out of sight, but you can still hear them. From the yelping, you know the trail is hot. The barks are getting louder—apparently the chase is coming your way. You have no idea if it is a bear, cougar or what, and you realize that there may be a chance to test your marksmanship. Maybe by this time you are wondering how you ever got mixed up in this deal. Finally you hear rifle shots in the distance and the yelping dims and stops. The successful hunter gives the time-honored signal, two quick shots in the air, and all the other hunters gather to look at the animal. For a while the excitement is at a fever pitch.

Those that shot and missed will have their reasons, and

the others like yourself, who never had a chance to fire the rifle, will have plenty of comments. Being a greenhorn hunter, you will ask a few questions and generally be an onlooker. The hunt will be good for plenty of stories later.

Fishing season was from late spring to the dog days in mid-August. Then a green moss developed in the creek beds and there was no more fishing until the fall rains cleared out the moss. The fish in Goose Neck and Mill Creek were native trout. The creeks flowed through dense brush and deep canyons, then out into open country through farms and ranches. The inaccessible spots in the streams gave the trout places to propagate, and there were always fish available.

Clarence and I had hazel or willow poles, with a line tied to the small end, and a plain hook. To carry our catch we strung them on a willow stick with a fork at the lower end to keep them from slipping off. In the spring our bait was angle worms from the garden, and in summer we caught grasshoppers in the fields or crawfish in the stream beds.

If you care to try it, here are a few suggestions. If an angle worm is your bait, thread the worm on the hook to cover as much of the hook as possible, leaving a loose end. If it's a grasshopper, put the hook through the center of the body, from one side to the other. While you are doing this, he will probably spit brown stuff on your fingers, but pay no mind, you are out fishing. If you use this method for grasshoppers, when they hit the water they will start wiggling, and Mr. Trout knows this is for real. For crawfish-tail bait, use the whole piece, and put the hook through the center. In the summer this is the most effective bait—I prefer it over grasshopper or any other.

When you approach the stream, be careful to keep completely out of sight of the trout in the water. They have sharp vision—any unnatural movement, especially human, and they are gone. If you can't find a bush, tree or rock to keep behind as you come up on the stream, you may have to crawl on your belly, keeping your head down. When you are close enough, throw the baited hook in the water. If you have followed these suggestions and there is a fish nearby, you will probably get a strike. Keep a tight line, and don't try to "horse" this type of fish out of the water, or you may lose him. In a few minutes he will tire and slow down, then you can bring him in.

Wherever fishing is concerned, tall tales are in order. The fish get bigger and more numerous with each retelling, but no listener is too concerned about accuracy. We figured there were a lot more fish caught around the stove at the country store than ever came out of the streams.

In the fall, salmon would swim up the streams to deposit their eggs. Where the stream ran through a populated area, sometimes a dog would hear the salmon splashing and would go to investigate. Soon he would be in the water, wrestling a fish around, and finally he dragged it out onto the bank, where he had a feast. There is something about the flesh of a salmon that makes a dog deathly sick—he can't eat anything, and lies around looking terrible. He probably wishes he could die, but he doesn't, and finally recovers. As long as that dog lives, he will never again go near a salmon. When people in the community had a bad experience with a product, they had an expression, "I've been salmoned."

One day in June the subject of fishing was bandied about by a group of men, including an elderly bachelor, Mr. Nathan Blair. I listened carefully, and decided that Mr. Blair knew what he was talking about. When the rest of the men had left, I mentioned to him that, if and when he was planning on a fishing trip, I would like to go along. He replied, "All right, you and Clarence can come with me the day after tommorow to Cedar Creek."

Cedar Creek was a branch of Mill Creek deep in the

mountains. We started about six, and walked up the logging camp road, then up Cedar Creek to a spot Mr. Blair knew well. It was a long hike and we were traveling light, with only our fishing gear, a frying pan, a small can of lard for frying the catch, and a fresh loaf of bread Mother had sent along.

Mr. Blair set the pace, and the walking was good until we reached the spot where Cedar Creek branched off from Mill Creek. Here there was only a trail, and we had to travel single file. We followed the trail until it opened into a wide grassy area. This was where we were to start fishing.

Suddenly a band of mountain grouse flew into a nearby tree. Mr. Blair drew his revolver and brought down one of the big birds with one shot. While Clarence and I were wondering what we would do with the bird, Mr. Blair told us he would give us a lesson in mountain survival. We were all eyes and ears.

With a sharp stick and his bare hands, Mr. Blair dug a deep, wide hole near the creek. We brought water from the creek in the fry pan, and he made a mud paste in the hole. We had no idea what this was all about, but he told us to make a fire, while he removed the head, feet and entrails, but not the feathers. Mr. Blair immersed the bird deep in the hole, and worked the mud into the feathers with his hands. When the bird had a thick coat of mud, it was larger than a football. Mr. Blair spread out the fire and laid the mudded grouse in the center, then raked the coals over it.

We fished nearby, returning occasionally to add wood to the fire. Mr. Blair was an old hand at the fishing business and we watched all his moves closely. After two hours or so, Mr. Blair's fish-basket was filled with trout, and he said, "That's it, boys. Let's go and see how our grouse is coming along."

I was not too sure about this cooking experiment. I had visions of charcoal, ashes, dirt and feathers in the eating.

Mr. Blair spread the coals, removed the ball of baked mud, and let it cool for a few minutes. Then he broke off a piece of the coating. Mud, feathers and skin all came off in one piece. The meat was well done, so he continued peeling off baked mud and put the clean cooked bird in the fry pan. He tore off chunks and handed them to each of us. This was a new experience for Clarence and me. When I tasted that roast grouse, it surpassed all my expectations for tenderness and flavor, and along with my mother's fresh bread, there could never be a meal to compare with it.

It was a fishing trip we would long remember—we got a lesson in fishing, and in survival in the mountains.

Socializing

People had to make their own entertainment in our community. Farms and ranches were isolated and people's daily work kept them in their own homes and fields, so folks grabbed any chance to get together that came along.

Evening get-togethers at home were popular. Several families would gather for an evening of card games like Seven Up, Pedro, Solo or Five Hundred. For the men it might be penny-ante poker or dominoes, and often there were checkers contests.

For the younger set, if space permitted, there were parlor games like Miller Boy and Farmer in the Dell. If parents were out of earshot, the boys promoted the game of Post Office, which always ended in one of the boys kissing one of the girls. There was a great deal of blushing and feigning resistance on the gal's part. When the mother found out that Post Office had been the game the daughter got a lecture.

Almost any excuse would do to get people together, and we passed up no opportunity. One day our friend Mr. Nathan Blair made a sensational announcement to the folks gathered at the store. He had bought an Edison phonograph! It was a deluxe model that could play both two- and four-minute records, and it was the first phonograph in Buell.

I was "sharped up like mashed potatoes" and ready for the Saturday night dance.

Mr. Blair's announcement created considerable excitement, and he agreed to bring the machine to the local schoolhouse for an evening of entertainment. A date was set and there was a big turnout. Mr. Blair had records of the latest songs of the day, *Red Wing, Pony Boy, By the Light of the Silvery Moon,* and other late numbers, sung by Ada Jones, Billy Murray and other songsters. To operate the Edison, Mr. Blair cranked up the large spring inside the cabinet, then put on one of the wax cylinder records and released the control lever. The first sound coming out of the horn was like something frying on the kitchen stove, followed by a monotone voice giving the name of the song and the singer, then the slowly enunciated words, "Edison Record," with more frying noises and, finally, the singer's voice. If the large spring was not wound tightly enough, the sound slowly ground down to a dismal stop. There would be laughter and wise-cracks until Mr. Blair could again wind up the spring. This remarkable music box made such an impression that Mr. Blair often filled in intermission times at social functions with his Edison.

The all-time favorite social event was the occasional Saturday night dance. It got wide publicity and the crowd came from near and far by horseback, horse and buggy or on foot. We gathered at the Russell Jones home on the Mill Creek Road about two miles from the country store, because they had a big dance floor with room for a crowd.

The younger generation went to considerable trouble getting ready for the big night. The young swain had to spend some time in the washtub scrubbing off a week's layer of grime, then scrape the stubble off his chin, trot out the mail-order suit and apply the flatiron, and generally get "sharped up." The young miss, and especially the not-quite-so-young miss polished up her charms with a curling iron heated in the chimney of a lamp. What gal wanted to be a wallflower all evening?

When folks arrived at the dance, Clarence Olmstead, the fiddler, would strike up a two-step, and follow it with a waltz, three-step, polka, scottische and quadrille numbers. One night the fox-trot appeared on the floor, and this was an eye-catcher. When Fiddler Olmstead needed a break, he was relieved by Herman Leonard with his harmonica. Fiddler Olmstead was rewarded with a fee of five dollars for his services, collected from the men present at the rate of fifty cents a head. Harmonica Herman received appreciation only, no cash. He was sort of the master of ceremonies, running the show.

At these public dances it seemed there was always a shortage of the feminine gender and a surplus of manpower. The crowd would be a mix of neighborhood families and the unattached swains, eager beavers and some older lonesome bachelors and a few old maids and widows—regular or grass widows (divorced). It was here that the unattached male could ask the idol of his dreams for a dance, and let the chips fall where they may.

A few times during the evening the master of ceremonies would announce "Ladies' Choice." The wives would be looking up their husbands and the young Lochinvars who had been giving the belle of the ball the rush act would learn their actual rating, because she would ask her favorite for the dance. This could be quite a blow for some eager fellows. The girls came with their fathers and mothers and were well coached on what nice girls did, so they would not hesitate to turn down a request for a dance if a young man's reputation was not of the highest order.

If a fellow didn't luck out on the "Ladies' Choice," he still had a chance. The master of ceremonies would announce a "Tag Two-Step" or a "Tag Waltz." This was a windfall for the timid male. Now he had an open field. If the apple of his eye was dancing, he could tap her partner on the shoulder and he got the gal. Of course, there was always the risk that another guy might tap him on the shoulder, then he would be out, but at least he had reached first base.

Often folks brought their families, and there was a room provided where the small fry could be bedded down as the evening wore on—and I do mean "wore on" because the music would start at eight o'clock and sometimes go on until dawn, with a break at midnight for coffee, cake and gossip. The saying was, "It's never late until two, and then it's too late." Clarence and I didn't stay around to find out about that—it was a two-mile walk home, and the chores had a way of coming around early on Sunday morning.

When a farmer or rancher built a new barn it was another excuse for a public wing-ding. The dress was strictly rural, with men in denim overalls and the gals in gingham. The lighting would be lanterns hung from the beams and the seating would be bales of straw around the sides of the dance floor. The floor was rough lumber and had to be heavily waxed for dancing.

Some of the men would have a jug or two of hard cider stashed around at convenient places in the new barn just in case there was a slowdown in the dancing. Hard cider was known for its kick—worse than a Missouri mule. It was fortunate for the community morals that not too many new barns were built, since barn dances did not have a very high rating with certain of the church-going folks.

From time to time there might be a special occasion, a wedding, church event or political meeting, that required formal dress. For these occasions the Man of Distinction and the Fashionable Lady would get rigged out in their best, "soup and fish." This decking-out was quite a project for either sex.

For the gentleman the first garments would be an undershirt and a pair of open-front drawers with loops at the top edge on each side for the ends of his suspenders, to prevent the drawers from coming down. The next item would be the white hard-front shirt, buttoned up in the rear. A celluloid collar was attached at the neck with a collar button front and aft. This type of collar was popular and practical because when it got dirty a damp cloth would restore it to service. To get the celluloid collar installed with a bow, string or necktie took a bit of dexterity. To add glamour to the front of the shirt a row of pearl-headed struts were secured down the center. Then the man would install a colorful garter on each sleeve above the elbow. These garters always seemed like excess baggage to me, because sleeves don't come down.

Next came socks, held up by a pair of Paris garters, then the tuxedo pants with suspenders, and patent leather shoes. Over all that went the scalloped-front vest and either a swallow-tail or knee-length coat, and a derby, plug or beaver hat.

The Fashionable Lady had to have an hourglass figure at any cost. To get it, she had to be cinched up in a steel-staved corset to the smallest possible diameter in her mid-section. She called upon an assistant to pull the drawstrings of the corset tighter and tighter—to get the tightest possible cinch the assistant put a knee against the lady's backside.

To prevent the steel staves in the corset from showing through a thin blouse or dress the lady wore a chemise covering her from the shoulders to below the corset. She hitched her stockings to the garters at the bottom of the corset front and back. Next came a pair of bloomers with elastic at the waist and knees. Then a starched petticoat and the silk, cotton or satin "Sunday best" dress. Her footwear was a pair of high-topped shoes laced up with shoestrings or a button hook.

The sky piece could range from a floppy wide-brim job to a small conservative model, all decorated with ribbons, artificial flowers or ostrich plumes. To keep the hat from blowing off in the wind, she inserted long

OUR GRAND ASSORTMENT OF CORSETS ARE UNSURPASSED.

We Guarantee Every Pair for Elegance of Fit and Wearing Qualities.

Our immense business and satisfied customers is sufficient proof that we sell the kind that pleases. WE WANT YOUR WAIST MEASURE, NOT YOUR BUST MEASURE.

OBSERVE THE FOLLOWING RULES in taking your measure: If you measure with corset on, deduct 2 or 2¼ inches from waist sizes as shown on tape; this allows for spread of lacing in back. For example, if waist measure is 23 inches over corset, order size 21. If you take actual body measure, without corset or underclothing, you should deduct 3 or 4 inches, depending on how tight you lace. For example, if your waist measure is 25 inches without corset or underclothing, your size would be 21 or 22.

Allow 15 cents extra if you want a corset sent by mail.

No. 62900 FLOWERED SATEEN STRIPE DRESDEN CORSET, long waist and medium figure, made of fine heavy drill, double front and side steels, 5-hook clasp and lace edging. Made in black or drab, covered with small flowers in contrasting colors. Sizes, 18 to 30. Price, each 50c

No. 62902 LONG WAIST, medium figure, 5-hook corset, French patterns made of good corset jeans, six side steels, boned bust and handsomely flossed, a corset made to retail for $1.00, and good value at that price. Colors, drab or white. Sizes, 18 to 30. Price, each 70c

No. 62904 S., R. & CO.'S NURSING CORSET. 5-hook reinforced clasp. Made of good corset jeans, entirely new principle, as it is easily adjusted, with patent snap button, and will permit use of nipple without the slightest inconvenience; very pliable over sensitive parts; a boon to mothers. Boned bust; strong jean girdle; two side steels. Color, drab only. Sizes, 18 to 30.
Price, each 75c

No. 62906 KABO NURSING CORSET. 5-hook, long waist, medium form. Constructed on scientific principles, improved snap glove fastener opening, well corded front and bust, English sateen, single side strip. A corset that is sure to give entire satisfaction. No brass eyelets. Colors, black, white or drab. Sizes, 18 to 30. Price, each 95c

No. 62908 LONG WAIST, MEDIUM FORM, 5-hook. This is a corset made of fine French Coutil strips of French sateen, with silk edging. Moulded on a perfect French model; stayed with double girdles at the waist line. The bones and steels are made with a protecting covering for the ends, which prevents cutting through. A perfect fitting garment that will give entire satisfaction. **Equal to the $1.50 kind elsewhere.** Made in white, drab and black.
Sizes, 18 to 30, price, each $0.90
Sizes, 31 to 36, price, each 1.15

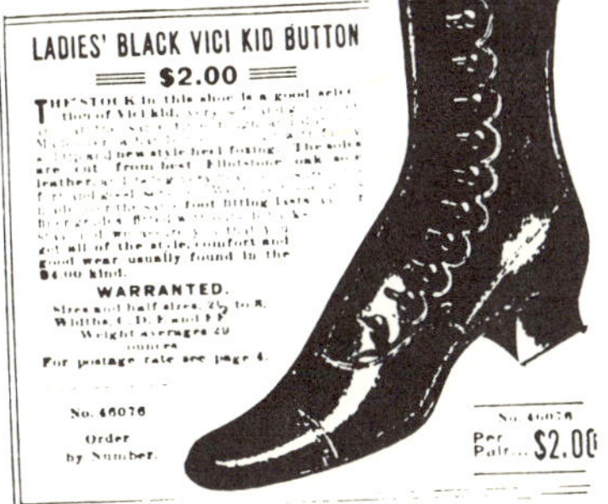

Celluloid Cuffs.

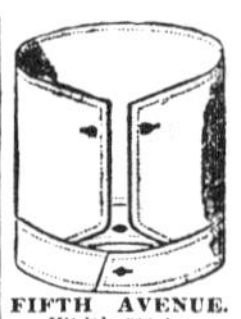

No. 50116 Style Fifth Avenue, Celluloid Cuffs. Sizes, 9½ to 11½.
Price, per pair......... $0.25
Price, per dozen....... 2.70

FIFTH AVENUE.
Width, 3¼ in.

No. 50117 Style Excelsior Celluloid Cuffs. Sizes, 9 to 11¼.
Price, per pair $0.25
Price, per dozen 2.70

Do not forget size when you order collars and cuffs.

EXCELSIOR.
Width, 3½ in.

NOTE.—Dozen rates apply where half dozen or more of the same kind of collars or cuffs are ordered.

Celluloid Shirt Front.

No. 50118 Celluloid Shirt Front, interlined, medium length.
Price, each $0.30
Price, per dozen 3.25

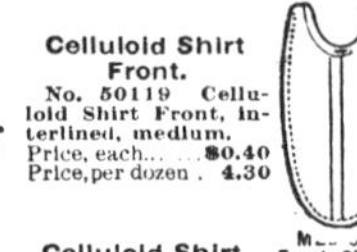

SHORT.
Front 7 In.
Width 6 3/4 In.

Celluloid Shirt Front.

No. 50119 Celluloid Shirt Front, interlined, medium.
Price, each.... $0.40
Price, per dozen . 4.30

MEDIUM.
Front, 9¼ in.
Width, 7 in.

Celluloid Shirt Front.

No. 50120 Long Shirt Front; length, 13 in., width, 6⅞ in.; made of extra quality celluloid, interlined. Price, each $0.50
Price, per dozen 5.30

When collars and cuffs are ordered sent by mail, always include extra stamps for postage. If by mail, postage on Collars, extra, per doz., 14 cents; each, 1 cent; on Cuffs, per doz. pairs, 20 cents; per pair, 2 cents.

Men's Rubber Bosoms.

No. 50121 Men's Rubber Bosom, 9¼ inches long, medium length. Price, each.................. $0.60
Price, per dozen........................ 6.70

White Rubber Collars and Cuffs Made with Smooth Luster Surface.

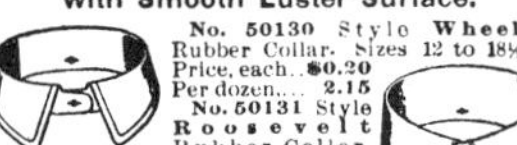

No. 50130 Style Wheeler Rubber Collar. Sizes 12 to 18½.
Price, each.. $0.20
Per dozen.... 2.15

Wheeler.
Front, 2 in.
Back, 1¾ in.

No. 50131 Style Roosevelt Rubber Collar. Sizes, 13½ to 17½.
Price, each.. $0.20
Per dozen... 2.15

Roosevelt.
Front, 2¼ in.
Back, 1⅞ in.

No. 50132 Style Miles Rubber Collar. Sizes, 12 to 18½.
Price, each $0.20
Per dozen. 2.15

Miles.
Front, 2 in.
Back, 1⅞ in.

No. 50134 Style Funston Rubber

Funston.

Suspenders and Braces.

No. 50400 Men's 1½-inch Elastic Web Suspenders. Dark or medium colors, fancy patterns, metal grip, back, braided ends and **strong wire buckles.** Per pair...8c
Per dozen pairs ..90c

No. 50402 Men's Fancy Silk Embroidered Suspenders. 1½ inch elastic web, medium colors, with braided ends and drawer supporters. **Nickeled** cast-off **buckles.** Handsomely embroidered with silk in assorted patterns.
Price per pair.. $0.15
Per dozen 1.50

No. 50400

If by mail, postage extra, per pair, 5 cents.

Berlin Back Suspenders.

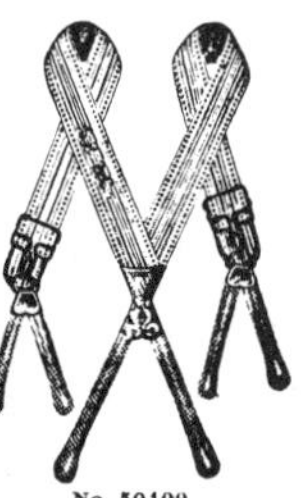

No. 50404 A Great Favorite. Made from heavy, strong 1½-inch elastic web, cushioned back. Assorted colored patterns. Extra strong non-breakable clasp and buckles. Full length.

Per pair.. $0.25
Per dozen, 2.70

If by mail, postage extra, per pair, 5 cents.

No. 50404

OUR NECKWEAR DEPARTMENT.

MEN'S AND BOYS'.

For Ladies' Neckwear see Notion Department.

IT IS QUITE POSSIBLE to buy good neckwear at a low price, but it is never possible to be satisfied with poor neckwear. In asking your careful consideration of this department, we need only say that **the goods are good and the prices are right. If you buy of us and do not find that this is so,** we are only too anxious to have you return the goods at our expense and **we** will refund your money.

Men's Silk Teck Scarfs, 19 and 25 Cents.

No. 50151 Men's Silk Teck Scarfs in large assortment of stripes, plaids and floral designs; also plain black silk or satin.
Price, each $0.19
Per dozen 2.10
If by mail, postage extra, each, 3 cents.

No. 50152 Men's Fine Silk Teck Scarfs in large assortment of floral, Persian, plaid and stripe effects. Also all white.
Price, each....... $0.25
Six for 1.35
Per dozen 2.70
If by mail, postage extra, each, 3 cents.

Excellent Value at 35 Cents.

No. 50153 Fine Brocaded Silk Teck Scarf, of the latest design and shape. Large assortment of light, medium and dark colors in new patterns. Also plain black silk or satin.
Price, each....... $0.35
Three for 1.00
If by mail, postage extra, each, 3 cents.

No. 50155 Men's Fine Silk Teck Scarfs. At this price we furnish a scarf which for quality and style is the best. Full width bands, best linings. The latest assortment in grouped stripe, Persian effect and plaids. **Strictly reliable high grade goods.** Give color preference and we can please you. Also plain white.
Price, each.... $0.45
Three for 1.28
Per dozen...... 5.00
If by mail, postage extra, each, 3 cents.

Men's Handsome Silk Teck Scarfs.

No. 50156 Medium dark and light evening shades, latest new shape, in great variety of designs. **Persian, Floral Plaids, Etc. In new Effects and colorings. All are made in strictly first-class manner, wide band and fine linings. An exquisite present.** Each scarf put up in beautiful box.
Price, each.......... $0.55
Three for........... 1.50
Dozen................ 6.00
If by mail, postage extra, each, 10 cents.

No. 50157 Our new style Teck Scarf, made to hook in the back. Small knot with wide aprons. A stylish strictly high grade scarf in large assortment of new silks.
Price, each.............. $0.45
Per dozen................ 5.00

hatpins through the crown of the hat and through her braided hair. Sometimes these hatpins were alleged to be useful for the lady's self-defense, though I never knew anyone who had to use one. In summer time, the outfit was topped off with an elaborate parasol and white gloves.

When a lady walked with this long flowing dress she had to hold it up with one hand to keep it out of the dust—but she also had to be careful not to hold it too high and expose her ankles. How a lady finally got through a hot summer day, or any other day, with this straight-jacket on is a mystery. What a relief it must have been for her to get out of it!

The picnic at the end of the grammar school term was another big event every year. All the wives in the neighborhood tried to out-do each other in bringing goodies to eat. Tables set up in the school yard groaned with the load of food, and it was all help-yourself. After you were completely stuffed, and could not eat another morsel, along comes Mrs. Smith or Mrs. Jones, urging you to try some of her specialty. At this point you do not care if you never see food again, but she insists—to refuse would be an insult. It is a big strawberry shortcake with a blanket of whipped cream between each layer and another blanket on top—you're stuck. It will be agony for most of that day.

There were events that we looked forward to every year, like the county fair and the national holidays. They provided entertainment for weeks, not just during the event, but as a topic of conversation before and after.

Memorial Day was the first of the national holidays. Ceremonies were held at the Buell campgrounds, where the covered platform stage was hung with colored streamers and seating was arranged for the crowd. Families from all the nearby neighborhoods came, and Civil and Spanish-American War veterans. It was always a solemn occasion, with a Pledge of Allegiance to the

Flag, band music, patriotic songs and a reading of the Gettysburg Address. Sometimes a state politician would come to deliver a speech, and sometimes this responsibility was handled by a prominent man in the community. After the ceremonies and visiting ended, some of the families went to the cemetery to put flowers on graves.

The Fourth of July called for a three-day celebration in Sheridan. It was the main get-together event of the year for families in nearby communities. Since we could only go for one of the three days, we always traveled to Sheridan on the Fourth, when most of the best celebrating was done.

Late in June large bright posters had appeared all over town ballyhooing the plans for each day of the celebrations. The anticipation was hard to take, but the Fourth finally arrived and Clarence and I were up early that day to get the chores done quickly. We set off on the seven-mile hike, each with a sandwich in our pocket and some money to squander (abut thirty-five cents for me and fifty cents for Clarence).

The parade started at 10:30, rolling down Main Street. The Grand Marshall, in the lead, sat on a beautiful white horse equipped with a shining silver-studded saddle and bridle. The Grand Marshall wore white buckskins, white riding boots, and a Stetson. Behind him were the Sheridan band playing patriotic tunes, a "prairie schooner" covered wagon drawn by a team of oxen, a group of Indians from the Grand Ronde Reservation, and prominent local citizens and clowns.

When the procession arrived at City Park, the Master of Ceremonies made a speech of welcome, the band played, a lady sang the National Anthem, and soon the fun began. There were contests of skill and endurance, like the custard-pie eating contest, the soda-cracker eating contest, the cross-cut saw log-cutting contest, and various races. My favorite was the automobile race. It was not a race for the highest speed. Instead, the last car to cross the finish line was the winner. If a car stopped moving it was out. It seemed that almost everybody who owned an automobile in all the towns around Sheridan entered the race, some decked out in long white duster coats, caps and goggles. It was exciting to see them line up at the start in their Ford, Maxwell, Nash, Overland, Studebaker, Willys-Knight, Pierce Arrow and Stanley Steamer cars. The whistle blew and they started to roll, slower and slower. Soon one would stop and it was out. The crowd really got into this act, shouting, laughing and telling the drivers what to do, until finally the last car crossed the finish line to the cheers of the crowd.

After that it was the baseball game—the Sheridan team against a team from a nearby town—and then, in the evening the fireworks and a street dance. Clarence and I tried to take in everything, but the day always went too fast. There was a seven-mile walk between us and the chores. Our final squander was at Thompson's Ice Cream Parlor where we each spent a dime on a dish of vanilla. Then we were on our way, with plenty of stories and conversation for our friends.

Summer was a busy time for farmers and ranchers and soon after the Fourth socializing had to give way to tending and harvesting crops. Entertainment was low-key until September.

Early in September folks would come together again for the Polk County Fair, held in Dallas on a Thursday, Friday and Saturday. People came from all over the area to exhibit the fruits of their labors.

For Clarence and me to get to the fair, we usually had to make arrangements to go with a family from the neighborhood. We could never go as a family because either Father or Mother had to be at the store to take care of the mail. So, we often got involved in the confusion of getting a family with several children off to the fair. The mother and daughters had packed the picnic dinner into baskets the night before, ready to go into the wagon in the morning. If two or more families were going as a group, dinner had to be worked out among the women-folk to avoid duplications. It was necessary to take dinner along because the only available public eating places were the Dallas Hotel or the Gail Hotel dining rooms, and at twenty-five cents a head, who could afford to feed a large family?

In the morning the action had to start by four, and the chores, breakfast, and dishes had to be done, then everybody got polished up in their best outfits. What with getting several excited children organized, then getting the horses harnessed, hitched up and on the way by six-thirty, no wonder mothers got grey early in life.

The trip to the fair was always exciting, full of new and old scenes—a new barn, a house recently painted, a tract of land cleared or other changes in the landscape. These things generated plenty of questions and conversation, but there was plenty of time for answers and discussion while traveling at the terrific speed of about three miles per hour.

When we finally reached the fair grounds, as soon as the wagon could be parked and the horses tied to the back, everyone took off to see the exhibits. Interest was especially keen if a son or daughter had an entry in one of the exhibits. Everyone was keyed up and anxious to see if a prize, a ribbon or honorable mention was displayed. Many of the young folk had spent considerable time on their 4-H project, and it was quite a thrill to see a blue ribbon on your work.

Bringing the 4-H Club to Buell had been the county school superintendant's idea. He had come to the school to explain the program and encourage the students to start 4-H projects. He did his work well and the students had a sales pitch that was difficult for their parents to turn down, so the 4-H Club went over in a big way. During the summer the various projects excited a lot of interest and conversation at the store. Some of the students soon discovered that it was a bigger undertaking than they had realized, but the pressure was on. Their parents were involved as well as other people in the neighborhood. What parent wanted his son or daughter to chicken out and be known as a quitter? As a result, there were almost no washouts.

Now, at the county fair, all the time and effort put into the projects paid off in blue ribbons and other prizes, as well as the excitement of having an exhibit at the fair.

Later everyone went off to make the rounds of the other exhibits, and to see the band, the merry-go-round and Ferris wheel, as well as the games of chance and other entertainments. Despite the stalls selling lemonade, soda pop, ice cream, peanuts, cotton candy and Cracker Jacks, everyone knew to be back at the wagon at noon for dinner. At twelve o'clock everyone was present and accounted for.

The women brought forth the baskets with the picnic spread while the men watered the horses and put oats in their nose bags. When the yell came, "Come and get it!" there was no hesitation. Soon the food was passed around, self-serve, seconds encouraged. Then the women who had brought their specialties came around suggesting you give this or that a try, until you were stuffed to the eyeballs. That was dinner at the county fair.

With dinner over, there was time for one more quick look around the fair to check back on a particularly interesting exhibit and make sure you hadn't missed anything. About three o'clock it was time to head for home. As usual, chores and supper were waiting.

Each year another kind of entertainment came to Buell: the Doctor Hizz Medicine Show. A front man would come through the community, making arrangements to use the Woodmen of the World Lodge Hall and putting up posters on fences, buildings, and at the country store. The posters extolled the merits of the Doctor's wonderful remedies and advertised the "free" entertainment.

Hop-picking crew, 1905, Jeff Davis Hopyard on Gooseneck Creek. Clarence is in the center of the front row.

Doctor Hizz arrived in a colorful covered wagon and set up camp at the campground. The Doctor was a distinguished-looking fellow with a goatee and white hair, and above all else he was an expert salesman and a master of crowd psychology.

He started the show in the Lodge Hall at 7:30 pm, with a warm welcome to the crowd, and introduced his two assistants. He launched into stories of the miracle cures his remedies had made, then he performed a few magic tricks and interspersed jokes with his silver-tongued sales pitch. He would come forth with packages of his product, and send his assistants out into the crowd. They started down the center aisle hawking and wisecracking and soon someone bought their offering. The hawker took the money and shouted to the Doctor on the stage, "Sold out again, Doc, change for a twenty." This went on until there were no more buyers for that product, and Doctor Hizz produced another cure-all and started over again. When the crowd's interest began to cool, Doctor Hizz thanked them for their interest and congratulated them on their purchases. By morning he was long gone, headed for the next place down the road.

At hop-picking time we had a double opportunity: we could combine socializing with the chance to earn a few extra bucks. Late August or early September people came to the big hopyards in the area to harvest the spongy pinecone-like hops from the long row of vines. The hop picking crew was made up of a wide assortment of people, including families, young people, widows, old maids and bachelors. Many people considered hop picking as their vacation, to renew friendships or make new friends and to beef up their finances. Some families came from far off and camped in cabins or tents provided by the grower.

In the mornings, and again after dinner at noon, the whole crew started picking hops at the same time and usually picked down the rows in a fairly close formation.

If one row had slow pickers, the foreman would assign part of the row to fast pickers, so they would all arrive at the ends of the rows at the same time. Sometimes a song would break out in one section of the crew and another section would join in. When folks weren't singing, there was plenty of conversation back and forth among the rows.

Every evening there would be a gathering around the campfires, with more singing and fun. Anyone who had a special talent had a chance to show it off here to people he didn't see every day—a fresh audience. Everybody who played a musical instrument brought it along at hop-picking time, to help liven up the evenings.

After all the hops were picked, the next day was payday. All the pickers came to the grower's yard where tables were set up. When the last picker was paid off, a wagon load of watermelons iced down in straw arrived on the scene. Everybody ate watermelon until they could eat no more, and went home with happy memories of hop picking time.

When the church or school needed funds for a special project, they raised money with an oyster stew supper on a Saturday night. One woman in the neighborhood would brew a large kettle of oyster stew with skim milk and several cans of oysters, seasoned with salt and pepper. Someone brought the oyster crackers, and others would furnish bowls, utensils and napkins. The men brought the kettle to the church and put it on the heating stove. As soon as the crowd had assembled the entertainment by the grammar school students would start. When it was over all the women's names were placed in a hat. As the hat was passed around, the men would pick out a name and make a contribution. The name he picked would be his oyster stew eating partner. When the names were selected and the stew was ladled out supper was underway, with conversation in full flower. When all the folks were stewed, the ladies who had made the investment in oysters and oyster crackers were reimbursed and the proceeds announced.

Public auctions always brought out a big crowd—no one can resist a bargain. These generally came in the fall after crops were harvested. A rancher or farmer would decide to retire or sell out and wanted to dispose of his equipment and household effects, and the auction sale was the answer. It got wide publicity with printed notices posted on fence posts, along the roads, and at the country store. The notices announced the time and place for the auction, and listed the major items to be sold, with a grabber at the end of the list, "and many other articles too numerous to mention." It was a sales pitch that was hard to resist, including an added attraction: free lunch at noon. The auction was the topic of the day at the country store.

Almost everyone could find an excuse to attend the auction—if not a real or imagined need, at least they could go to meet their friends. Mr. Millard F. White, the auctioneer, was another well-known attraction. He was an amusing entertainer with a ready supply of jokes and stories—some of which needed to go to the laundry. He was a good judge of values and a shrewd student of crowd reactions. He could make the buyer feel that he was his friend.

The show started at ten in the morning with the items of lesser value. Auctioneer White knocked these off quickly at low prices, a clever piece of psychology that attracted the attention of the crowd and created the impression that things were going at bargain prices. The major items were held back until the "cats and dogs" were unloaded. Sales moved along rapidly until noon, when time-out was declared for the free lunch. The menu was the same at all auctions, and often the supplies were bought at the country store. Lunch was a ten-pound wooden box of soda crackers and two five-pound rounds of Tillamook cheese, plus coffee brewed in a wash boiler

Postcards for every occasion — postage one cent.

and served in tin cups. The auctioneer's assistants sliced the cheese and set the box of crackers on a table in the yard. They served coffee with a long-handled dipper. One swig of that potent brew was enough for some folks—it was as strong as horseradish.

During the noon hour the auctioneer mingled with the crowd. Neighbors had a chance to compare notes, meet old friends and make new ones. Promptly at one the auction started again and moved rapidly until everything was sold. As the auctioneer completed each sale a clerk collected the money or made arrangements with the buyer for payment. The auctioneer's compensation was a percentage of the selling price, so he made an earnest effort to get the highest possible price. Whenever the crowd started to lose interest, the auctioneer brought them back into the fold with one of his jokes.

These auctions were planned to finish about four o'clock, so that folks could gather up their purchases and get home in time to take care of the chores. Auction day was always a happy occasion. It was good for a couple of days of conversation afterwards at the country store.

With fall came Halloween, and Halloween was a night for devilment and mischief. There was no trick-or-treat for the little folks since houses were too far apart. There was no shortage in the trick department, though. The teen-age boys in the neighborhood took care of that. They were careful not to damage or destroy property, but they made sure that the results of their fun were seen by as many people as possible.

The first stunt was to climb up on the grammar school roof and toll the school bell. When folks heard the bell they knew Halloween was under way. Another favorite prank was to take a buggy or piece of farm equipment apart and reassemble it on the ridge of the roof of the owner's barn. The lumber flume, which was elevated and visible from the road, was another ideal place to decorate with farm equipment. The most popular stunt of all was tipping over the Chick Sales—the small square building that every home had out back. The boys would come in from the rear of the property and, when the mission was accomplished, escape by the same route. In the morning the folks had a surprise—and a problem.

All these pranks were rehashed for several days, then no more Halloween for another year.

Soon it was Thanksgiving time, and it was a holiday that was celebrated in our community in the spirit it was intended for. We gave thanks for the bountiful harvest and counted our blessings. The custom in Buell was for two or more families to get together for the big dinner every year, and alternate year by year making the dinner. The visiting family would bring a special dessert to add to the festivities. After dinner everyone sat around visiting and digesting for a while—when a feast like that has gone down your dumpling path, you aren't thinking about supper for a while. Still, everyone headed for home early, since, holiday or not, there were chores to be done.

The community celebration of Christmas centered around the school. The school teacher made plans with several of the parents in the neighborhood to set up a tree at the school. Men would bring in a suitable fir tree and set it up, and the wives and school children would make up long strands of popcorn on a strong cord and other tree decorations, including candles. One of the fathers would volunteer to play Santa Claus on the big night.

On Christmas Eve the candles on the tree were lit and everyone came to the school. Parents put presents on or under the tree, with a minimum of explanation to the little folks. Then came a program of songs and recitations and sometimes a Christmas play by the grammar school students. Soon there would be a rap at the front door, and all the children held their breath as old Santa Claus came in, bowing and greeting everybody, with special attention to the small fry. He distributed the presents, adding a personal touch to each one.

When the excitement over the presents ebbed, the teacher announced that the children could have the popcorn strands on the tree. What a scramble! Soon parents and children were homeward bound.

We worked hard all year round in our farming community, but we were also experts at having a good time. Socializing brought families and neighbors closer together and made hard work easier.

Going to Town

A trip into town was always a treat. Father went into Sheridan almost every week to get supplies for the store, but for Clarence and me it was catch as catch can, when there was no conflict with school or other jobs. When the big day came, we were up with the chickens to get the chores and breakfast over, and to get decked out in a fresh clean outfit, with shoes shined and hair combed. As soon as the mail was dispatched at eight o'clock we were on our way.

We made the seven-mile journey in every kind of weather, year round. The roads were dirt, except where a layer of creek bed gravel had been applied here and there, and they were dusty in the summer and in some places axle-deep in mud in the winter. We rode in an open wagon, with the sky for a roof. On a winter day, with the wind and rain blowing in your face and water dribbling down your neck to make a puddle where you sit on the hard wooden seat, after a few hours you might think your posterior was paralyzed. Sometimes we had hot bricks wrapped in paper to keep our feet warm, but this was strictly a one-way ticket—on the return trip they were stone cold. Still, Father never got any gripes or bellyaching from Clarence and me. When it came to going to town, we were always cocked and primed and ready to go.

In the winter sometimes we would pass crews of men working on the road, laying logs six to eight inches in diameter side by side over the mud in the swampiest places. Father explained that the road was maintained by the people who lived along it. With a system called a "pole tax" each neighbor contributed one day's work or a fee of three dollars.

I always had a lively interest in the advertising signs we saw along the road. The local paper, the *Sheridan Sun* was a weekly and many people did not subscribe, so local merchants and national marketers resorted to signs painted on barns and fences. The fences were about five feet high and made of six-inch-wide boards, with spaces between the boards equally divided. The painter painted the area around each letter in the sign. The result was a unique and interesting sign.

The national companies put up large, colorful signs on the sides of barns, where they could be seen for long distances. They advertised Sherwin-Williams Paints—"Cover the Earth," Wrigley's Spearmint Gum—"The Flavor Lasts," Grandpa's Wonder Soap—"For Hands and Face," and tobacco brands like Bull Durham, Mail Pouch and Peerless. The representative of the company who approached a farmer for permission to paint a sign on his barn might have thought he was dealing with a country hick. The salesman found out fast that the farmer was not so dumb—often he got his whole barn painted free.

On these trips to town I got a chance to try out my knowledge of livestock, the result of my many hours with my nose in the Chicago Livestock Food Company's catalog. Father was a patient teacher and was always ready to discuss the merits and weaknesses of each breed of livestock. As we passed farms and ranches, I could pick out the breeds of cattle, horses, sheep, goats and fowl that we saw. Sometimes Father and I would disagree about a particular breed, but there was always the dog-eared catalogue ready to settle the dispute when we

A free paint job for the barn.

got home.

Along our road we passed miles and miles of fences, some built of split rails and some of boards, that separated one farm from another and one field from the next. One day the thought struck me—who decides which owner is responsible for keeping up the fence? This was a toughie and Father did not have the answer right away. A few days later at the store I put the question to one of the local pioneer land owners. He told me that when a fence was planned, the owners started from opposite ends of the property line and walked toward each other. When they met in the middle, they shook hands and each agreed to build and maintain the fence for the stretch behind him. This was the accepted method, no lawyers involved.

On a spring day, you could almost tell where you were on the road with your eyes closed. The fragrance of wildflowers, clover and vetch in bloom in the fields, the scent of newly mown hay or flowering orchards was a treat. Sooner or later, though, you would pass a field or pasture where the farmer had spread the previous winter's accumulation of manure on the land, or a hogpen set too close to the road. If it was a hot day it might get rather pungent, but it was all part of the trip, and when we got out of it we appreciated the fresh air.

As we approached Sheridan the houses were closer and closer together, and the farms and ranches were behind us. Soon there were people walking around, and plenty of traffic on saddle horses or in buggies and wagons. We were in town!

If we had freight to be shipped by rail, our first stop was the freight depot. In a small town like Sheridan, the freight and passenger depot was one long building parallel to the tracks, and each train was a mix of passenger and freight cars. The agent at the freight depot would take whatever Father wanted to ship and write him a bill of lading, one copy to keep and one to mail to the man who would receive the cargo. If we were to pick up freight, Father paid the shipping charges and we loaded the freight on our wagon.

If we had a coop of chickens, a calf or a few pigs on the wagon we delivered them to the slaughter house at the far side of town. The place was set well back from the main road at the end of a lane. From a long way off we noticed the scent and knew it wasn't coming from a perfume factory. We delivered our load and the foreman gave us a receipt, redeemable in cash at the meat market. I was always glad to get away from this smelly place. I wondered about the men who worked there all day—what kind of a reception did they get when they came home at night?

Our next stop was the meat market to redeem the receipt. This was the place to buy fresh beef, pork or mutton and dressed chickens. The floor was covered with sawdust and the butcher wore straw cuffs and a straw hat. He was always friendly and you felt he was giving you a superior cut of meat. When he had cut and weighed meat for a customer, he added a free soup bone. That bone was the beginning of many a fine meal. My mother would cook it slowly in a big iron kettle for a long time, then add garden vegetables and let it simmer—what a flavor!

The market also sold smoked ham, shoulder, side meat, salt pork, sausage, headcheese, corned beef, lard, baloney and salted salmon. By the time we finished our business with the butcher it was usually noon. Father bought a ring of baloney and we walked across the street to the department store for ten cents worth of bulk crackers for lunch.

We drove to the public yard to unhitch and water the horses, then put oats in their nose bags. If the weather was bad we drove into the livery stable for the comfort of man and beast. When the horses were munching their oats, we sat on the wagon tongue and ate our baloney and crackers. By the time we had finished eating our lunch the horses had finished, too, and we started making our rounds of the merchants in town to gather supplies for the store and farm.

Going around with Father to the bank, stores and shops was always exciting. For a young lad from the country to be handshaking the president of the bank or the owner of a store was no small fish fry. None of my peers rated anything on this level, and when we got home they got an earful.

It was the stores' policy to treat a customer like a guest. There was no self-service. If a customer wanted information or was ready to make a purchase, there was a clerk there to ask, "May I help you?"

The Sheridan Department Store was the biggest store in town. On the main floor were departments for provisions, dry goods, men's and women's clothes, furniture and other household and farm items. At the rear of the building there was a large heating stove with benches around it, where folks would gather. It was a meeting place for people from the various communities, a headquarters for rural folks. Women waiting for their husbands to finish their business put the time to good use exchanging news.

The offices were upstairs, at the rear of the store, overlooking the main floor. Cable lines ran from the various departments up to the office, and whenever a purchase was made, the salesperson put the cash or credit invoices into a small metal cage and pulled a cord attached to a spring arrangement. The cage shot up the cable to the office, where clerks made change or approved credit. The clerk put the change back into the metal cage and sent it flying back to the point of sale. I never got tired of watching this show.

In addition to the main store, there was a warehouse near the railroad station freight depot stocked with farm, ranch and industrial equipment and machinery, including wagons, buggies, plows, harrows and other heavy hardware. Whatever a farmer or rancher needed, he could count on the Sheridan Department Store to supply it.

The bakery, down the street from the department store, was a delight shop. Its cases were stuffed with cookies, doughnuts, cinnamon rolls with icing on top, decorated cakes and loaves of fresh bread. Cookies were one cent each, ten cents a dozen; doughnuts and cinnamon rolls were two for five cents or twenty-five cents a dozen; bread was five cents a loaf or six loaves for a quarter. The bakery did not sell pies—a woman made her pies at home. The cinnamon rolls were my idea of living, especially if we happened to be in the shop when they were hot from the oven.

The confectionery and ice cream parlor was the sweet shop of the town. It was a rare treat for Clarence or me to visit this store—usually we had to pass it by. They sold all kinds of chocolates and fancy candies, displayed in showcases. There were jelly beans, gum drops, lemon drops, wintergreen and peppermint lozenges, and "farmer's mix"—several flavors and shapes of hard candy. All these bulk candies sold for twenty cents a pound or four ounces for a nickel, and there were several kinds of stick candy in big square glass jars. For the swains with romance in mind there were ribbon covered boxes of bon-bons. The store had colorful wrapping paper to serve this trade.

The soda fountain and ice cream parlor were the confectionery's magnet attractions. This was where people gathered. The soda jerk put on quite a show, tossing a scoop of ice cream and catching it on a cone. The soda flavorings were displayed in tall round bottles with shiny nickel-plated tops. A soda, with flavoring syrup and fizz-water, cost five cents. If you wanted an ice cream soda it set you back ten cents. A young man who wanted to make an impression on a girlfriend might order a couple of sundaes, tariff fifteen cents each. If he felt especially affluent or the girl was hard to impress, he would go all the way—a banana split with three different kinds of ice cream, crushed fruit and toppings with a maraschino cherry on top. This cost twenty-five cents, and proved that he was a "big spender."

All this was much too grand for any ordinary occasion. Except for the Fourth of July with Clarence or perhaps an extremely hot day on trips to town with Father, my chances of getting into that confectionery were exactly zero. Father apparently felt there were more important things to be done in town than sitting on a soda fountain stool sipping a sody.

One of the best-maintained stores in the town was the drugstore — clean windows, clean showcases, orderly displays — everything ship-shape, including the druggist. Over the front door there was a signboard that proclaimed, "Pharmacy - Drugs - Prescriptions - Toiletries." That shook me—in our neighborhood people avoided using the word "toilet" and I never expected to see it advertised in public.

The druggist filled prescriptions for the two doctors in town, and sold many kinds of patent medicines, ointments, and pills. He had some medical knowledge and often made helpful suggestions as to the quality or effect of some particular product. The shop also carried perfumes and a few other items, all displayed neatly in show cases or on counters.

At the rear of the main room there was a partition with a smaller room behind it, where the druggist kept certain supplies. There was a small one-way mirror in the wall, so that when the druggist was filling a prescription, he could watch what went on in the main room. This back room was where doctors replenished the drugs they carried in their small leather pill bags when making house or hospital calls.

The druggist was a prominent man in the town, active

in community affairs, and his store had an atmosphere unlike the other retail stores.

The barber shop was more than a place to get a shave and haircut. It also offered shoeshines and baths for men. In addition, it was the news headquarters for the town.

Regular customers had their own shaving mug and brush on the barber's shelf. Each mug had the owner's name or initials embossed on it. When the man's turn came for the chair, the barber draped a large chair cloth around his neck and pushed the chair into a reclining position. Then he put a Turkish towel wrung out of hot water around the man's face to soften up the whiskers. While the customer was baking in the hot towel, the barber took down his mug and whipped up a heavy soap lather with the brush.

At this point the barber might put on a show for the benefit of the chair warmers or bystanders. He would sharpen the straight-edge razor on a leather strap hanging from the back of the chair, whetting the blade on the strap. If he did not time his moves perfectly, the razor strap would be sliced and ruined. When he worked up to a fast stroke, the razor made a loud slapping noise and looked as if it were rolling on the strap. It was an eye-catcher.

When the barber finished stropping the blade, if he still felt like showing off, he would hold a single long hair at one end and move the razor down it, slicing the hair lengthwise. I suppose this is where we get the expression "splitting hairs."

After all this, it was almost a letdown to watch the barber shaving the customer, wiping the soap and whiskers on the wet Turkish towel. When the tonsorial services were completed, the barber collected his fifteen cents for the shave and called out, "Next gentleman, please."

In each community there were a few crusty old characters who lived far back in the hills. Because of the distance to town and the time involved, they seldom presented themselves at a barber shop. When one of these fellows did appear, the growth on his chin and the fur on his head were enough to give an experienced barber a shock. The man also made use of the bathtub in the small room at the back of the shop. He certainly got his money's worth—fifteen cents for a shave, twenty-five cents for a haircut and twenty-five cents for bathtub, hot water, soap and towel. This type of customer was not sought after, but barber shops were open to the public.

Every once in a while we got a real treat on our trips into town. In winter, when the weather was rough, drummers from wholesale firms would ask Father to meet them in Sheridan, to save them the long trip to Buell in a rented buggy. They always took us to the leading hotel for dinner, and as far as I was concerned, we were going top-drawer. In the hotel dining room, the ordinary tables were covered with oilcloth, but the commercial table where we sat had a linen cloth and napkins. It was raised on a platform above the main floor, and the folks eating at the regular tables gave us the eye. When the drummer signed the check and handed it back to the waiter, I was impressed. . . Father, Clarence and me going for free! In the center of the table was a large bowl of oranges, and the drummer invited me to have one. I never passed up that opportunity. The orange was a rare treat and I ate the whole thing—peeling and all.

The drummers were personable men, and brought new ideas and interesting products to our store. They usually carried large catalogs with pictures and information about their offerings, as well as samples. It was always exciting to look through the drummers' catalogs. Those stories of the traveling salesman and the farmer's daughter never had any truth to them, by the way. The farmer's daughter was much too closely chaperoned by her parents, sisters, brothers, and Aunts Bessie and Matilda to ever have the good fortune to meet a traveling drummer.

When we had finished our business in town, our last stop was the flour mill. We filled all the remaining space in the wagon bed with sacks of flour, bran, shorts (a ground whole grain for livestock) and dry corn. Everything in the flour mill, including the miller, was covered in a fine white dust that sifted from the gristmills. We tied a tarpaulin over our wagon load, and headed for home.

These trips to town were more than joy rides for Clarence and me. They were a liberal education in rural living and commercial dealing that has served us both well.

The Gentle Sex

"A man's work is from sun to sun—a woman's work is never done." Whoever said that must have known my mother.

A woman had to be modest, feminine, and highly moral. That was the attitude, and no one thought of changing it. Yet, a woman worked as hard as a man—in some ways harder—caring for a large family, helping in the fields, and generally doing whatever needed to be done.

A mother's constant concern was her family, which often included four or more children and sometimes an aged grandparent. During that era, grandparents often lived out their remaining years with their sons' or daughters' families, helping the mother to bring up the children. The family always came first.

Working conditions for the housewife were not entirely ideal. She had to draw water from the well, light the house with coal oil lamps and cook on a woodburning stove. The housewife's day started about five, to have breakfast

OUR NEW 1901 MODEL ACME PRINCESS COOK STOVE

Made With Porcelain Lined Reservoir at $12.50 to $14.25. Made Without Reservoir but with Extension End Shelf at $9.20 to $10.90.

WE OFFER THE ACME PRINCESS AS AN ENTIRELY NEW STOVE FOR 1901, MADE IN OUR OWN FOUNDRY FROM THE BEST MATERIAL THAT MONEY CAN BUY, BY THE MOST SKILLED MECHANICS THAT WE CAN EMPLOY.

Our Prices Are Only the Cost of the Material and Labor with but Our One Small Profit Added.

AS ADVERTISED 8X18 SIZE. $13.95.

FROM THE ABOVE ILLUSTRATION, ENGRAVED FROM A PHOTOGRAPH, YOU CAN FORM SOME IDEA OF THE APPEARANCE OF OUR NEW ACME PRINCESS.

END US $1.00 AS A GUARANTEE OF GOOD FAITH, state whether you wish the stove for coal only, or both coal and wood, and we will send the stove to you by freight, C. O. D., subject to examination; you can examine it at your freight depot nd if found perfectly satisfactory, exactly as represented, one of the handsomest reservoir cook stoves you have ever seen, and equal to stoves that your torekeeper at home sells at almost double the price, pay the freight agent the balance and freight charges. The freight will amount to next to nothing as ompared with what you will save in price. The stove weighs about 310 pounds and the freight for 200 miles will be about 50 cents; 400 miles, 75 cents; 00 miles, $1.00; 1,000 miles, $1.50. Greater or lesser distances in proportion.

OUR BINDING GUARANTEE. With every stove we issue a written binding guarantee, y the terms and conditions of which if any piece or part gives out by reason of efect in material or workmanship we will replace it or repair it free of charge.

WE GUARANTEE SAFE DELIVERY Every Acme Princess stove will be carefully crated, and we guarantee it to reach you in the same perfect condition it leaves us, and if upon arrival any piece or part is broken or missing, we will replace the same free of any expense to you.

WE WILL ALWAYS HAVE A SUPPLY OF PARTS. If in the years to come any part breaks or gives way we will be prepared to supply you with such part on a short notice, for we shall always have a stock of Acme stove castings on hand which we can supply promptly,

THE ACME PRINCESS BURNS HARD COAL, SOFT COAL, COKE, WOOD OR ANYTHING FOR FUEL.

GENERAL DESCRIPTION. THE ACME PRINCESS is made with very large flues, cut tops, heavy cut centers supported by post, heavy covers, heavy linings with very heavy sectional fire back, large bailed ash pan, slide hearth plate, nickeled outside oven shelf, ouch feed, oven door kicker, nickel plated panel on oven doors, nickel plated name plate on front door, nickel plated door knobs, heavy tin lined oven doors.

When ashes are removed from under the oven they are scraped into the hearth, avoiding all possibility of spilling the ashes on the floor when cleaning e stove. The Acme Princess is furnished with a lifter, shaker and scraper for removing the ashes from under the oven.

It is fitted with a large porcelain lined reservoir, as shown in the illustration, and is furnished on a large, handsome rococo pattern base. **It has every p-to-date feature** of every high grade reservoir cook stove, every improvement up to 1901, and is one of the best reservoir cook stoves on the market.

If you do not burn coal at all, make your selection from Catalogue Nos. 74809 to 74817.

Prices do not include pipe or cooking utensils. See pages 902 to 903.

ALWAYS STATE WHICH FUEL YOU WISH TO BURN.

PRICE LIST ACME PRINCESS COOK STOVE, **WITHOUT RESERVOIR.**

Catalogue Number	Size	Size of Lids	Size of Oven, Inches	Size of top not measuring shelf, Inches	Size of Shelf, Inches	Height, Inches	Pipe to fit Collar, Inches	Fire Box for Wood, Inches	Weight, Lbs.	PRICE
4906	7-16	No. 7	16x14½x10	22x29½	22x7	26½	6	16½	212	$ 9.20
4907	8-16	No. 8	16x14½x10	22x29½	22x7	26½	6	16½	212	9.25
4908	8-18	No. 8	18x17 x11	24x33	24x7	28½	7	18	254	10.85
4909	9-18	No. 9	18x17 x11	24x33	24x7	28½	7	18	254	10.90

PRICE LIST ACME PRINCESS, WITH PORCELAIN LINED RESERVOIR.

Catalogue Number	Size	Size of Lids	Size of Oven, Inches	Size of top including Reservoir Inches	Height, Inches	Pipe to fit Collar, Inches	Fire Box, Inches	Weight, Lbs.	PRICE
74910	7-16	No. 7	16x14½x10	22x40	26½	6	16½	265	$12.50
74911	8-16	No. 8	16x14½x10	22x40	26½	6	16½	265	12.55
74912	8-18	No. 8	18x17 x11	24x44	28½	7	18	310	13.95
74913	9-18	No. 9	18x17 x11	24x44	28½	7	18	310	14.25

$13.95 IS THE POPULAR SIZE, THE 8-18 SIZE; WEIGHS 310 POUNDS AND WE OFFER IT AT $13.95.

ready in time for the manpower to be in the fields by seven.

Men's work was usually hard physical labor, on the business end of a shovel, pitchfork, grub hoe, or axe. Breakfast had to sustain them for five hours until dinner at noon, so it was a substantial meal, and required some planning and work. Dinner was much the same situation, and for supper, family members needed no appetizer—they could put away a creditable volume of food, because after supper more chores were waiting. For the women, after each meal there were the masses of dishes, pots, and pans to be washed in one dish pan, then rinsed in another, and dried with a towel. There was no drainboard—where would the water drain to, with no indoor water pipes?

Cooking a meal was a major operation. Mother needed vegetables from the garden or roothouse and eggs from the henhouse, and there had to be wood to stoke the stove and fill the woodbox. Of course, that's what children are for, to fetch the items Mother needs, and Clarence and I were pressed into service.

Meat for most meals was pork, because it could be preserved in salt brine or salted and smoked, and we had our own supply. Beef or other meats would spoil too quickly. We brought the ham, shoulder, or side meat (later called bacon) in from the smokehouse, then Mother would parboil it to remove the salt. The boiling went on until a white foam collected on top of the water. Mother drained the water and fried, roasted or baked the meat. If she was frying, the aroma coming from the kitchen would be enough to turn a finicky eater into a glutton.

Cooking over a wood-fired stove is a tricky business—too much or too little wood in the small firebox, or the wrong kind of wood, or a damper opened too far, and the meal can be a disaster. A wood stove has a personality of its own, and needs careful attention, or the family may go hungry. Keeping the woodbox filled was a job Clarence and I could have lived without, but we were stuck. The woodbox had to be neat, not just a pile of sticks, because Mother needed fir for kindling, ash for general cooking, and oak for baking close at hand.

The stove's firebox was small, because a large one would make the temperature hard to control. This meant Mother had to be very careful of the sort of fire she built, and had to stoke it frequently. She kept the firebox about two-thirds full, and added one stick of wood at a time.

The other way to regulate the heat of the stove was with the draft control at the front of the firebox and the damper in the stovepipe. By opening and closing the draft and damper in different combinations, Mother could control the heat on the stove and in the oven. It was quite a skilled performance.

Please don't get the idea that women served only meat and potatoes. They took pride in their culinary skills and accomplishments. They canned many kinds of fruit and vegetables and they served a long list of their own specialties—pickles, relishes, pickled onions, sauerkraut, piccalilli, rhubarb-strawberry jam, apple and quince butter, jellies and mincemeat, to name a few.

My mother's piccalilli was a great favorite and always in demand. She would slice green tomatoes, onions and green peppers, then salt them down and let them stand overnight. In the morning she rinsed them with cold water, then sugar, celery seed, mustard seed, cloves, cinnamon stick, allspice berries and cider vinegar went into the pot. Mother cooked it all until it was crisp-tender, and put it up in jars. When a neighbor stayed to dinner, the specialties of the house were on display on the table, and Mother never had to twist anybody's arm to try her piccalilli.

Desserts were another way to show off a woman's talents. Each lady had her specialty, and tried to out-do her neighbors. Apple pie rated number one, but there were also custard, coconut cream, mince and berry. A standard-size pie would be cut into four pieces and served with a bowl of whipped cream or a pitcher of heavy cream. When it came to cakes, layer cake with a blanket of whipped cream between each layer was the usual, but when strawberry season came along there would be a layer of strawberries in the whipped cream—this was what the menfolk talked about.

There was more to good eating than the cooking—if a woman wasn't good at preserving food, her family could get hungry during the winter. Women took pride in keeping their larders well stocked. The roothouse and buttery would be filled in summer and at harvest time, so there would be no shortages in the cold months.

The roothouse was a cool building, with double walls insulated with sawdust. Wide shelves extended the length of the building, holding the harvest of fruits and vegetables from the garden and orchard. The bottom shelves held the heavy squashes and pumpkins, then there were potatoes, turnips, rutabagas, carrots and beets on the middle shelves, and apples and pears at the top. Apples have to be stored carefully, in a single layer if possible, so they won't bruise and spoil. One bad apple can spoil many others. Parsnips were a different story—we left them in the garden, since they got sweeter after a good freeze.

Mother's canning operation would include the other vegetables and fruits that wouldn't keep in the roothouse, like tomatoes, beets, small onions, peaches, prunes and plums. She stored these in the buttery off the kitchen.

In case you get a sudden yen to can fruit sometime, here is how it was done at our house. The glass jars were washed and boiled, ready for filling. Then we washed, peeled and pitted the fruit (a good job for a kid like me), and cooked it with water in an open kettle. Mother added the "simple syrup"—one part sugar, two parts water. The kettle required constant attention and stirring to keep the fruit from burning and here again, Junior was pressed into service.

When the fruit was cooked, we dipped or poured it into the glass jars and sealed them with rubber rings and zinc screw caps. Sounds simple enough, doesn't it? But maybe in getting the hot fruit from the open kettle into the two-inch opening at the top of the jar, you will get some experience. You are holding the glass jar in one hand, and with the other hand you dip the hot fruit into the jar. Soon the jar gets hot and if your dipper touches the top of the jar or you overfill it, fruit and syrup run down the side onto your hand, or you may spill some on the hot stove or on the floor—either way you have a sticky mess to clean up. At this point I want to wish you well and good luck with your fruit canning.

Keeping eggs could be a problem. They were a vital part of nearly every meal, and a family needed eggs all year round. The hens wouldn't cooperate, though—they produced more than enough in summer, then slacked off at moulting time in October, and there wouldn't be many eggs during the winter. We solved the problem with the "water glass" method of preserving eggs. Father bought liquid sodium silicate from a store in Sheridan, and Mother boiled a quart of the solution in three gallons of water. When it cooled, she poured the sodium silicate solution over the eggs in a big earthen crock. It sealed the pores of the eggshells, and they would keep for six months or more and taste just like fresh eggs. After several months the yolks began to break down, but it didn't matter because by then the hens were producing again.

The daughters in a family got plenty of practical experience helping their mothers—experience that served them well later in life. There being no daughters in our home, Clarence or yours truly assumed that role. Both of us have benefitted greatly from the lessons we learned helping our mother.

Women had a special project for almost every day of

the week. In many homes Monday was wash day, Tuesday was ironing day, and Wednesday was bread-making day. Often Clarence or I would lend Mother a hand with these jobs when she was called away to tend to the store or post office.

For wash day it was draw the water from the well, carry it into the house and pour it into the washboiler to heat on the kitchen stove—don't forget to keep stoking the stove with wood. When the water is hot, pour it into washtub number one, with its washboard and bar of soap for rubbing and scrubbing the clothes. When the clothes are scrubbed, crank them through the rubber rollers of the clothes wringer into tub number two for a rinse, then back through the wringer. Put the white clothes into another tub for bluing. This third tub has a small ball of bluing dissolved in it, so the water is light blue. Bluing keeps white clothes from turning yellow after several washings. Then crank everything through the wringer one more time and hang it on the line to dry. When you think of all this cranking of the clothes back and forth in and out of the tubs through the rubber roller, surely you can better appreciate the problem the hired girl is alleged to have experienced with her anatomy.

For a long time this was how washing was done at our house. Then finally Father worked out a deal to buy a washing machine at a wholesale price. No more leaning over for hours scrubbing clothes on a washboard. We had a new washing machine, the latest word in laundry. It had a vertical stick handle and a foot pedal at the lower end of the handle. When you pushed the handle, the pedal moved out, and when you stepped on the pedal, the handle returned to its original position. The movement in and out with the handle and pedal moved gears that turned an agitator inside the machine, moving the clothes around in the soapy water.

It didn't take me long to improve on that business of

No. 15368. The Peerless Wringer is the most popular wringer with high class trade, and we can not recommend it too highly. The distinguishing feature of the Peerless is the clamping device which has recently been imitated by other makers, but comparison shows the imitation is only in general appearance and not in fine workmanship and finish which characterizes the Peerless. Has **guide roller, double gears** and rolls 10x1¾ inches; **warranted.** Price, each........**$2.00**

No. 15369. The Unrivaled Wringer. Desiring to give our customers a large variety of wringers to select from, we have added this first-class wringer to our line. The material for the frame is carefully selected from first-class lumber. Has guide roller, 2 top screws and swinging iron clamps. Rolls, 10x1¾ inches: **warranted.** Price, each..................................**$2.00**

Sad Irons.

These irons are so well and favorably known, we only refer to a few points. There are three sizes in each set. No. 1 weighs 4 lbs. and has one end rounded for polishing; No. 2 weighs 5⅛ lbs., No. 3 weighs 5⅝ lbs. Only the No. 1 size has one end rounded. The detachable handle is of wood and fits naturally to the hand without straining the arm or wrist.

No. 15336. Potts' Pattern Sad Irons in sets of 3, as described above, with one detachable wood handle and one sad iron stand. Plain polished. Price, per set.**59c**

No. 15337. Same as 15336, nickel plated. Price, per set..**64c**

No. 15338. Extra handles for above sad irons. Price, each..**8c**

No. 15342. Common Pattern Sad Irons, with face finely polished. Weights given are not guaranteed exact. They are the manufacturers' weights (so-called), and are as near as it is possible to make them.

Weight, lbs.,	5	6	7	8	9
Price, each,	$0.13	.15	.18	.20	.23

Sad Iron Stands.

No. 15343. Sad Iron Stands. bronzed iron. Price, each......... **5c** Per doz.............**54c**

Polishing Irons.

No. 15346. Troy Polishing Irons, with **perforated bottom,** nicely polished. Weight, 4 lbs. Price, each..............**30c**

No. 15347. Troy Polishing Iron with **smooth bottom,** nicely nickel plated. Weight, 4 lbs. Price, each.............**35c**

COD LIVER OIL.

Guaranteed Absolutely Pure. Highest Grade Made.

Look at Our Prices: Full Pint Bottles....$ .50 Per Dozen.......... 5.50

You will save one-half in price and get the best goods possible to put up if you place your order with us.

You can't afford to buy Cod Liver Oil unless you know it is absolutely pure.

If you buy from us you will have our guarantee and know it is absolutely pure and fresh, **imported direct from Norway,** in original packages, where it is prepared from strictly fresh livers, pure and sweet.

For Consumption, Severe Colds, Lung and Throat Troubles, NORWAY COD LIVER OIL should be taken regularly.

No. D1572 Per pint bottle............**50c**
Per dozen...............**$5.50**

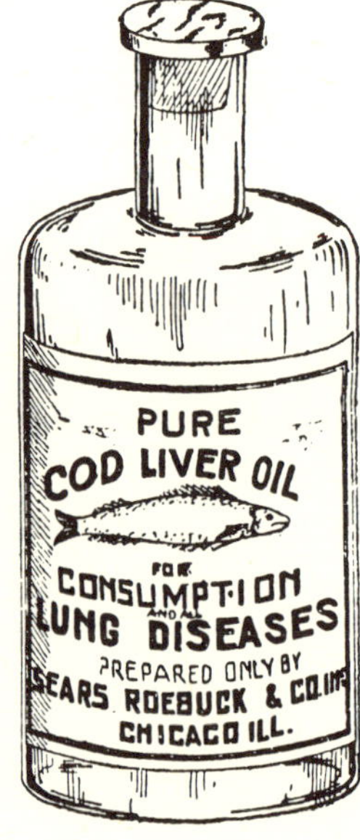

standing on one leg, pushing and pedaling back and forth. I sat on a chair with one foot high up the handle and the other on the pedal—it was the same as sitting down walking. This freed both my hands so I could read or, better still, play my harmonica. My repertoire consisted of such popular numbers as *Turkey in the Straw, Home Sweet Home* and *Irish Washer Woman,* an especially appropriate number for the occasion. Mother thought my idea was sharp, entertaining as well as helping her.

Even so, Monday was one day I could do without. But no loss without some gain—on Monday Mother cooked a New England dinner for noontime. She cooked meat and several kinds of vegetables in a big iron kettle, then spread the feast on a platter in the center of the table—let your conscience be your guide. That was the best thing that happened on Mondays.

Tuesday was ironing day for Monday's wash. Almost the entire wash had to be ironed with flatirons heated on the kitchen stove. It was another day of constantly stoking the stove firebox, and keeping a close eye on it to make sure the fire was low and steady, so the flatirons didn't overheat and scorch the clothes. The irons had a detachable handle, and Mother would pick up a hot iron and use it until it cooled, then put it back on the stove and pick up another one. On hot summer days, standing for hours ironing a basket full of clothes was no small workout.

Wednesday for many families was bread-making day, and if Mother could wedge it in, it was bread-making day at our house. My mother took as much pride in her bread as other women did, and the baking was often a subject of discussion. One long-running debate was over what kind of flour made the best bread. Some women favored flour made from hard winter wheat, and some preferred soft wheat flour. Whichever flour won out, the bread-making was an exacting operation. After Mother had all the ingredients mixed and the dough kneaded, she formed it into three loaves and let it rise at the back of the stove. Then she kneaded it down and put the pans back to rise again.

When the loaves were ready for the oven, Mother checked the firebox carefully—the temperature needed to be even throughout the baking. She used only hardwood in the stove for baking. Sticks of oak gave a good steady heat and burned down to long-lasting coals. When the baking was done, she took the loaves out and put them upside down on a bread board to cool.

How well I remember coming home from school in the afternoon and smelling the wonderful aroma of freshly baked bread! With a young lad's appetite, I could hardly wait to get a hunk off the end of one of the loaves, but at our house that was *verboten.* There was an unwritten law: Never cut newly baked bread. It had to be completely cooled. It was a tough rule, but I had to live with it. Sometimes it seemed that I would perish before getting that slice of bread. . . to me it tasted like cake. At meals the inroads on the fresh bread were severe. A layer of Mother's special jam on a slice was not too difficult to take, and sometimes just before going to bed we would have a treat: a slice of bread in a bowl of milk.

Medical help for our community was far away and expensive, so Mother had her own remedies for our problems. For burns she would bind a slice of raw potato on the surface of the burn, to stay until the potato turned black. When she removed the potato, the pain was gone. For a stubbed toe, a cut or an open wound, she would apply turpentine and a white cloth bandage. To remove a thorn or a wood sliver that was too deep to extract with the point of a knife blade, she would bind on a small slice of fat pork. In a day or two the sliver was out and on the fat pork.

If I got the "back door trots" her remedy was a quarter-teaspoon of grated nutmeg with an equal amount of sugar. Down it with water and the problem was solved. For the opposite problem, when I'd get off my regular routine, she would come forth with the castor oil bottle and fill a tablespoon full. I had to try to get it down. Then in the spring of each year, after the long winter and the lack of sunshine, it was cod liver oil to build up the blood. I didn't know which was worse, the castor oil or the cod liver oil, but I would rather take a whipping than go around for three days belching either one.

If there was anything worse than cod liver oil, it was sulphur and molasses, alleged to cleanse the blood, a must every spring. Sulphur and molasses also appeared if Clarence or I had a boil or a pimple. It tasted like a kill-or-cure remedy.

If I had a congestion in the chest I was in for the mustard poultice cure. Mother mixed dry mustard and warm water and spread the paste on a cloth to apply to the chest. Soon the heat began building up, which was supposed to break up the congestion. When it was almost cooking me alive, Mother removed the poultice and replaced it with a new batch. Frankly, I would rather have the chest congestion.

Parents were concerned with their children's schooling. Mother sometimes dropped by the grammar school while classes were in session, and she was the one we consulted for help with our homework. Even before we started school, Mother wanted us to learn German. In the evenings she would read from a German primer and write in a copy book, and we would repeat what she had done. Sometimes she sang songs in German, then in English. It was uphill all the way for her, because she was the only person in the neighborhood who could speak German.

If you know anything about the German people you know they are thorough in their work. The result was that both of the young Walkers absorbed some

German—if not the language, at least a lesson in persistence. Later, Kaiser Wilhelm and the war in Europe made the German language a no-no, so we didn't parade our knowledge around.

My mother was a resourceful woman, and managed to solve problems that would have stumped many people. When we first moved into the house at Buell the walls were badly insulated, and our first winter was a chilly one. Mother decided to do something about it, and she got her inspiration from the pile of wooden packing crates that accumulated at the store. Instead of burning them, she set Clarence and me to dismantling them, carefully, so as not to split the boards or bend the nails. When we had a sizable pile of boards and nails, we started nailing them on the walls in the living room, bedroom and kitchen.

After several days of matching and nailing boards, the three rooms were boarded up. Our next job was to tack up cheesecloth to hold the wallpaper paste. If you are not experienced in the art of wallpaper hanging, let me tell you how it's done. First, the flour and water paste must be the proper consistency, not too thin or too thick. Cut the rolls of wallpaper to the proper lengths and apply the paste to the back of the first sheet. You are now ready to hang wallpaper. Start at the top of the wall, pressing the paper to the cheesecloth, and work downward with your hands to press out any wrinkles and seal the paper to the cloth. The first sheet is easy—the rest may be a little more complicated! Remember to match the edge of the second sheet to the first, and don't forget to match up the design on the paper. As you are pressing out the wrinkles, be careful that the pressure from your hands is even, or the top will let go. Down comes the sheet, paste plastered all over you and all over the front of the paper. In the struggle to hold it off the floor and get it back in place the paste dries and . . . pretty soon you wish you had never heard of wallpaper.

Clarence and Mother had just about gotten to this point in our project when Dame Fortune smiled on the Walkers. A stranger rode up to the store on a roan pony, with a big black dog following behind. He spoke almost no English, but Mother recognized his accent and spoke to him in German. It seems he had just arrived from Switzerland, and his name was Karl Kasper. He had taken up a timber claim in Tillamook, and was on his way to pick hops in the central Willamette Valley.

The conversation turned to our project, and we discovered our good luck. Mr. Kasper was an experienced paper hanger, trained in the trade in Switzerland, and he took over the papering job. When he left two days later, the rooms had a fresh new look, and Mr. Kasper had provisions from the store.

All the women in our community kept busy, but my mother had more demands on her time than most. Besides the usual round of her household duties, she might have to care for the livestock, gather eggs, or tend her garden. On top of that, when Father was away or busy, Mother served the customers in the store. Whatever project she might have planned for the day, she had to be flexible, because anything might come up.

However, even my mother was not slaving all the time. Often a neighbor lady would bring her sewing and sit with Mother for a chat in the afternoon, or a couple of women would drop by the store to trade ideas and recipes, and maybe a little gossip. Being barely dry back of the ears, I was excluded from the gossip.

When Clarence and I reflect on the years at Buell, we are amazed at our mother's accomplishments. I believe the good Lord knew what he was doing when he gave the man the wide shoulders to provide and the woman the wide hips to bear the children. Without my mother in the picture, we could never have made a success of the store and farm, and our lives would have been dreary without her good humor and loving support.

Haying & Grain Harvesting

Hay and grains were important crops in our area, as feed for horses, cattle and other livestock, and as cash crops. On our farm we had several acres of hay every year, and Father, Clarence and I harvested it ourselves. On some of the larger farms and ranches, though, haying was a major operation.

At haying time on our farm, my first responsibility was to crank a grindstone and drip water on it, while Father or Clarence sharpened the mowing machine blades mounted on the sickle bar. If I did not keep an even turning speed, or drip the right amount of water on the grindstone, the blade would not sharpen properly, and I heard about it right away.

Oat and wheat hay are cut before the kernels at the top of the stalks are fully matured. The hay is cut when it is "in the milk," meaning that the kernels are not hard yet, and when you press one, it releases a white fluid.

In a small haying operation, a driver with a team of horses and a mowing machine cuts the hay. The mowing machine has two steel wheels about four feet in diameter, with steel cleats on the outside rims. The farmer puts the mower in gear and when it starts to move, the steel cleats dig into the ground. This provides the power to operate the sickle bar, which oscillates back and forth in a metal frame. It cuts the standing stalks of hay about two inches from the ground.

The farmer begins cutting at the outer edge of the field, and continues around the edge of the standing stalks until all the hay is on the ground in swaths about six feet wide. Here it will remain for a day or more to dry in the sun. When the hay is dry, the farmer uses a dump rake to collect the stalks and dump them in long rows, called windrows. We piled the hay in haycocks to cure about a week. At that point the hay is ready for the haymow, unless it is to be baled.

When our hay was ready, Clarence and I drove to the field with a team and wagon equipped with a hayrack. While Clarence pitched hay on the rack, I spread it to make an even load. When the hay was piled as high as Clarence could pitch it, we drove to the barn. If you ever ride on a load of newly-mown hay, it will be an experience you will not soon forget—the fragrance is delightful.

At the barn I climbed up into the haymow and spread hay around as Clarence pitched off the wagon. This being June, the temperature outside was in the high nineties, and with no air circulation in the haymow, it didn't take long to develop a sweat. Sometimes in the mid-afternoon Mother would appear with a cool pitcher of lemonade. She never got any backtalk or criticism on the quality of her lemonade. When our haying was finished, Clarence and I would help our neighbors with theirs, and earn a few dollars.

On some farms or ranches where there was more hay than the haymow could hold, the surplus would be baled. The baler crew parked the machine in the field of haycocks. A driver with a low skid sled moved the haycocks to the baler, where the hay was fed into the machine and compressed into a bale. A man called a wire puncher put three strands of wire around the compressed bale, weighed it, and recorded the weight on a tag. He placed the tag under one of the wires, then stacked the bale with others nearby, later to be hauled to storage or to market.

The power source for the baler was a team of horses driven around a circle about forty feet in diameter. The team was hitched to a long lever arm bar, connected to a set of enclosed gears at the center of the circle. These gears operated another bar connected to the compressing unit inside the baler.

One haying season Clarence and I worked with a baler crew. Because he was husky and had more clout, he rated the job of wire puncher, and his compensation was a buck fifty for a ten-hour day. My assignment was to walk behind the team of horses hitched to the long lever arm, piloting them around and around the circle. As the day wore on at any particular location, the dust got deeper and deeper where I had to walk. If there was a breeze, when I walked facing the wind the dust was so thick I could not see the team in front of me. On a day when the temperature was a hundred in the shade (and where could you find shade in a hay field?) this eating dust for ten hours was rough. My pay was a buck a day. Clarence did not have a rose garden, but at least he did not have the dust, and he didn't have to be valet to a team of horses three times a day.

Meals for the baler crew were at the farmer's or rancher's home where we baled the hay. Our sleeping quarters were in the stubble field with the sky for a roof. My position was at the bottom of the totem pole on the baler crew, but I was not going to be known as a quitter. I stuck it out for the season, until all the hay in the neighborhood was baled.

Harvesting grain was a two-phase operation—binding in late July and threshing in August. A binder machine cut the stalks of ripe grain and tied them into a bundle with binding twine. It carried the bundles along on a rack until there were six or more, then the operator dropped bundles in the stubble field. A second man picked up the bundles and stood them on the cut ends, leaning the tops together. When the bundles were standing together, it was called a "shock" of grain.

One day in late July Mr. Freeman, a local grain farmer, was at the country store talking grain harvesting with Father. He mentioned that he was about to start work with his binder and he needed a man to shock grain for a few days. He would pay a dollar fifty a day. I had never worked shocking grain, but Clarence had shown me how to do it, and how to prevent the bundles of grain from falling over. A dollar and a half was big-time dough, and I offered my services without delay.

Mr. Freeman took a long look at the twelve-year-old (at least I thought it was long), and finally said, "Young man, do you think you can cut the mustard?" I said, "Give me a try!" and displayed plenty of confidence. He told me to be at his place Monday morning.

I was standing at his gate at seven on Monday morning, when he arrived with his three-horse team hitched to the binder machine. He placed a small wooden jug of drinking water in the shade of the gatepost, and started cutting grain around the outer edge of the field. When the six bundles had collected on the binder rack, he dropped them in the stubble, where I picked them up two at a time and set them up. This went on for five hours until noon, with the sun pouring it on at ninety or more. The jug of water was put to good use.

I had trouble holding the jug high enough to drink from it. Mr. Freeman showed me how to do it with one hand, holding the jug on my shoulder. Later, whenever drinking water on a job was in jugs, I pulled this stunt—it was a hit.

At noon we unhitched the team and went to the barn to water and feed them, then headed for the house.

Mrs. Freeman was an excellent cook and the table was loaded with food, which was plenty O.K. as far as yours truly was concerned. After dinner a brief rest, then we were back in the grain field until six. When the horses were cared for and stalled for the night, I walked the half-mile home to my supper. I had no problems sleeping that night.

The grain was cut and shocked by the third afternoon. When Mr. Freeman handed me a five-dollar greenback, I forgot all about the three days of sweat and the warm drinking water in the wooden jug. That was the end of grain shocking for that season.

For about three weeks in August every year, the community turned to grain threshing. It was a sizable operation, with a crew of twenty-five or more people and a lot of equipment. A group of local farmers and ranchers had made the investment in the threshing equipment, and they recruited the crew, established the wage scale, decided on the fees to be paid for the threshing services, and operated the machines. Several of the owners worked as members of the crew.

The operation moved from field to field to thresh each farmer's grain. When a farmer had only a small amount to be threshed, the threshing crew brought it to a nearby field where the machine was already set up. The grain separator was a machine about fifty feet long and ten feet high, and it was powered by a huge self-propelled steam engine. There was a wagon with a water tank for the steam engine, six to eight bundle wagons, a cookwagon, and eighteen horses. When this procession moved along a narrow country road, with the big engine leading the parade, belching steam, then the long line of wagons, and two boys on horses bringing up the rear, it brought folks out of their houses to watch and wave. The threshing crew had returned!

The steam engine had a full-time engineer and a fireman. It required a supply of water and firewood at all

IRONSIDES AGITATOR SEPARATOR

BUILT TO THRESH, CLEAN AND SAVE GRAIN.

24 TO 40 INCH CYLINDERS

BELT MACHINE

RIGHT SIDE

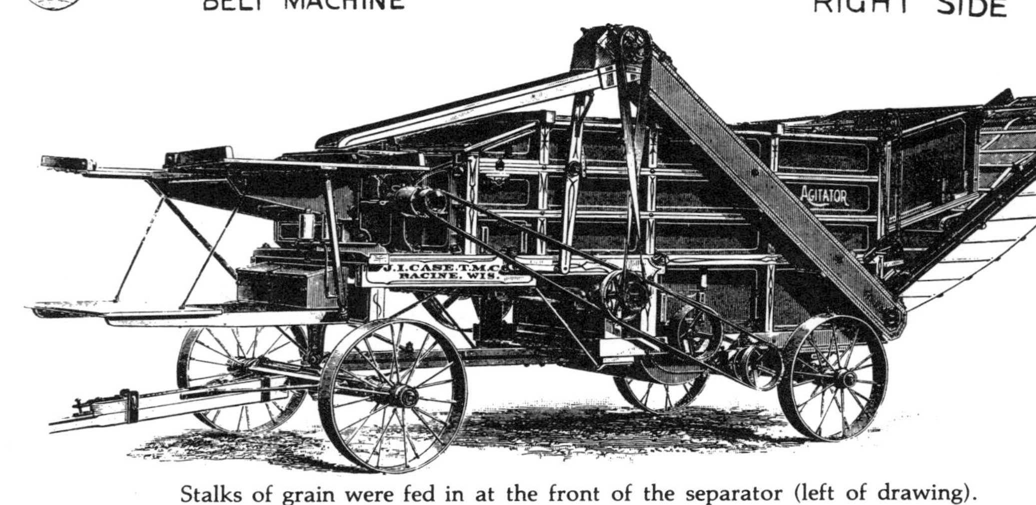

Stalks of grain were fed in at the front of the separator (left of drawing). Straw and chaff came out of the elevated chute at the right.

times. The water was pumped with a hand pump from the nearest creek or well into the tank wagon, then hauled to the engine and again pumped by hand into the boiler. Each farmer provided wood where his grain was to be threshed. The fields and the weeds along the road were bone dry in August, and everyone was on the lookout to make sure a stray spark did not ignite a fire.

When the separator was set up in a grain field, a belt about forty feet long connected the drive wheel on the engine to the large wheel on the separator. This turned a series of belts, gears, fans, and grates which separated the kernels from the grain stalks. In the field, bundle pitchers pitched the bundles of grain standing in the shocks onto wagons to be hauled to the separator. Here the wagon driver pitched the bundles onto a platform at the level of the intake chute of the separator. A man called a "bundle cutter" stood at each end of the platform and cut the binding twine from each bundle, then passed the loose stalks of grain to a man who pushed the stalks down a chute into a spinning cylinder of knives at the lower end. The knives shredded the stalks and released the kernels of grain, then the straw, chaff and kernels passed onto a tilted perforated tray, which vibrated. Most of the kernels passed through the holes in the grate, while a fan blew straw and chaff over to another grate, where any remaining kernels fell through.

The grain, now free of straw and chaff, poured into a metal tube and came out the lower side of the separator. Two men filled burlap sacks with grain, sewed the tops of the bags, and stacked them out of the way. The straw and chaff fell onto a moving canvas draper belt that carried it up into an elevated chute about twelve feet above ground level. The straw and chaff dropped out the end of the chute and fell to the ground, where it piled up. Two boys called "strawbucks," each riding a horse hitched to the opposite sides of a skid-sled, dragged the accumulation away into the stubble field. Later some of

The cookwagon — a mobile restaurant in the wheat fields.

Self-propelled steam engine.

the straw was used for bedding down stock.

Strawbucking was my job on the thresher crew. On each trip to drag away the straw, one of the strawbucks had to pass under the chute, with the straw and chaff pouring down. We got a shower of it in the face and down the neck. I just had to endure the itch and scratch in the August heat until I could get to the wash basin at the cookwagon for dinner or supper. The job included taking care of the horse, which meant I had to get up early to water, feed, and harness the beast. One season of this at one dollar a day, and I decided there must be an easier way to make a living than bucking straw.

Clarence fared better than I did. He had the job of bundle pitcher, with no straw and chaff down the neck and no nag to water and feed. Still, I did no squawking. I was glad to be earning the money for new shoes, clothes or school books.

The cookwagon crew was essential to the threshing operation. The men worked long hours in the field, and without plenty of good food there would be no crew. The same woman had the job of cook for several years in our neighborhood. Whatever she was paid, in my opinion it wasn't enough. She was up by four to cook for twenty-five or more hungry men on a wood stove in a wagon, and she produced three huge meals a day. She had a girl assistant and a roustabout man to help her, but she had the responsibility of serving the meals on time.

When all the grain in the neighborhood was threshed, the big steam engine, water tank wagon, separator, cookwagon and all the bundle wagon beds were stored in one farmer's barn until next year's harvest. The crew was paid and the men who had worked together for three weeks or more went back to their families. Many of them had worked together every threshing season for several years, and some were almost sorry when the job was finished. They would be there and ready when next year's threshing time came.

Logging and Lumbering

Lumber in Oregon, like corn in Iowa, has long been a major crop. For many years Portland has been considered the lumber capitol of the United States.

When my parents took over the store and farm, a sizable lumber mill had been established on Mill Creek, about two miles south of the store. In a few years the supply of timber near the mill was depleted, and the mill owners decided to expand their operation and establish a logging camp in the vast mountain forest six miles upstream on Mill Creek.

The first problem was to build a road through the forest to the campsite. In many places the road had to be carved out of the sides of the mountains. It was a single lane, and generally followed Mill Creek. When the road was completed, the construction crew could start building the logging camp.

First the crew cleared away trees and brush, then brought in lumber to build bunkhouses, a cookhouse, an office, sheds for tools and equipment, and barns for the horses. A large storage dam was constructed on Mill Creek to accumulate logs until the heavy winter rains brought enough water to fill the dam and float them downstream to the sawmill.

The logging company made arrangements with my

father to deliver provisions from the store one day a week. This is where I got into the action. Either Clarence or I would accompany Father on these trips. On the narrow mountain road there were only few places where two vehicles could pass each other, and our job was to walk ahead of the team to warn any oncoming wagon.

We started the six-mile trip early in the morning, and about four hours later we arrived at camp and unloaded at the cookhouse. Then we would meet the superintendent, Frank Riley. Mr. Riley stood six-feet four-inches, a hundred ninety pounds of muscle. He had the Irishman's smile and personality, but he was also one hundred percent logger. He could look at a tree and tell the board-feet of finished lumber it would produce at the sawmill, and he knew every phase of the logging operation.

When the camp was established, the owners bought a huge steam-powered donkey engine to move logs from wherever they were cut down to a central location, later to be moved with a team of horses over a skid road to the storage dam. The engine arrived by railroad on a flatcar at Sheridan. It was mounted on two huge skid runners, each three feet in diameter and twenty or more feet long. The job was to move it to the logging camp, fifteen miles away. The first nine miles were on country dirt roads from Sheridan to the sawmill, then six miles over the logging camp road. The assignment called for skill and experience, and Mr. Lee Ladd, a freight hauler from Sheridan, was selected. He owned two teams of Clydesdale draft horses, and he hired a pair of Percherons, about the same size as the Clydesdales.

Mr. Ladd directed the three teams of horses with one rein, called a "jerk line," with which he controlled the lead pair. It was truly a spectacle to see this lineup of horseflesh, with their harnesses trimmed with shiny metal decorations, pulling the big engine on its skids.

The procession moved slowly along the narrow road.

The donkey engine — the power source for moving logs.

When it passed a ranch or farm the family usually came out to watch—it was a sight not soon forgotten. There were some problems, though. Folks traveling the same road with their horses and wagons or farm equipment had real trouble if they needed to pass the donkey engine. Their horses had never seen such a monster in the road, and there were many runaways. Also, as the engine dragged over the dirt roads, a thin layer of wood rubbed off the underside of the skids and was embedded in the road. That summer many of the barefoot boys in the neighborhood came home with splinters. For a while folks were allergic to donkey engines.

When the procession finally arrived at the sawmill, Mr. Ladd and his horses returned to Sheridan and the second phase of the trip began. The engineer decided to move the engine by its own power to the camp. The cable on one of the big drums was unwound and anchored to a large stump or tree up the road. The engineer reversed the drum to wind in the cable, pulling the engine up to the anchor point. After several days of repeating this process, the iron horse delivered itself to the logging camp.

The steam engine was installed near a water supply, and a tall sturdy tree was selected as a spar pole. All the branches and the top of the tree were cut off, and a man called a "high climber" attached a large steel pulley at the top. The high climber specialized in this sort of job, and went from one logging camp to another installing cables and pulleys. The spar pole was anchored with cables to other trees around it. A cable from the drum of the donkey engine passed through the pulley at the top of the spar pole and on to the area where the trees were cut down.

The loggers used cross-cut saws nine feet long to cut down trees and buck them into the proper lengths for the sawmill. Sawing through a tree five feet thick takes plenty of muscle. When the tree was bucked up in appropriate lengths, men called "choker setters" attached the donkey engine cable to the end of the tree, ready to be pulled to the spar pole.

When a log was ready to be moved, the choker setters gave the signal to a lad called a "whistle punk," who sat on a high stump, where he could see over a wide area. The whistle punk jerked a wire that extended to the steam whistle on the donkey engine. One jerk, and the engineer started the cable drum and the log was on its way. Two jerks, and the engineer would slack off the pull on the cable so the crew could move the log around an obstruction or reset the choker.

In my opinion this whistle punk job was a real cream-puff, just to sit all day on a stump and yank that whistle wire. How could you do better than that—no dust, no sweat, plenty of food and good pay? If I could have gotten that job, I would have had it made, but it never came my way.

After the logs reached the spar pole area, they were dragged by a team of horses or mules to the bank of the storage pond. There a crew of men rolled them into the pond.

This system of logging was repeated until all the accessible trees suitable for lumber in the spar pole area were harvested. Then the superintendent selected a new location for the donkey engine and a new spar pole was set up.

When the storage pond was filled with logs and Mill Creek was at flood stage, they blasted the dam and water and logs rushed through the opening with a roar like thunder. Then one of the most dangerous jobs in all the logging operations began—riding the logs six miles downstream to the sawmill log pond.

Men known as "log drivers" took on this responsibility. It was the driver's job to ride the logs in the fast current, carrying a long pike pole to steer, guide, or maneuver the logs as they floated downstream. These men wore heavy leather high-topped shoes with caulks (short steel spikes) in the soles and heels so they wouldn't slip while riding the logs or jumping from log to log. The drivers walked on the logs, crossing and recrossing the stream, keeping the logs in the current.

It was dangerous work, and sometimes a driver might misjudge the distance of the jump from log to log, or might lose his balance and fall in the raging current. If two logs closed over him, there was no escape. In spite of the danger, there were men who followed this type of work from log drive to log drive.

The loggers were rugged men doing rugged work. When they came out of the camp, often they stopped at the country store to cash their checks and buy clothes, shoes, or supplies. Some of the men stayed at the camps for months at a time, and when they came out they would have a real grubstake—plenty of money. Some might go to Portland for a fling, and come by the store a week later, flat broke, on their way back to the camp to earn another grubstake. Men with families would sometimes come out of the camp on Saturday night and return on Sunday afternoon.

In general, the logger was something of a floater, moving from camp to camp. Often the labor turnover was high. The farmers and ranchers commented, "They have three crews—one crew coming on duty, one crew working and one crew leaving."

One way to help keep loggers on the job was to provide plenty of the best food around. The cook in a logging camp held a position of real responsibility. Whenever Father and Clarence or I visited the camp, we were invited to stay for dinner—I certainly wasn't going to make the cook mad by refusing.

At the entrance to the cookhouse there was a porch with a long table where there were buckets of water, washbasins, soap and towels. When the cook sounded the bell, the crowd came in. In the dining room was a long table with benches along each side that would seat twenty or more. The food was served family style—as soon as a plate or bowl was empty it was refilled, and let your conscience be your guide.

Conversation and stories circulated around the dinner table. The loggers' favorites were Paul Bunyan stories, and they got bigger and better with every re-telling. It seems that Paul was born weighing not seven or eight pounds, but seventy or eighty. His first scream was heard for a mile, and indicated that he would be a hero. His mother had to use a bed sheet for a diaper and a herd of cows could hardly supply enough milk. It is reported that Paul consumed a barrel of cod liver oil every three days—to me that proved he was brave!

The Ladies' Sewing Society volunteered to make a pair of pants for Paul. A sail maker donated a pair of mainsails, and a wagon builder contributed a dozen cartwheels for the buttons. Paul quickly grew to be ten times bigger and twenty times stronger than any other lumberjack.

One day, when Paul was looking out over the ocean, he saw some horns sticking out of the water between the icebergs. He jumped in, pushed the icebergs aside and pulled out a huge blue ox. The ox's horns were like the branches of a tree. Paul named his new pet Babe.

Far back in the forest there was a giant stand of timber where the trees were growing upside down. This posed a problem, because the loggers had to stand on their heads to chop down the trees, and they had to hang on to the ground to keep from falling into a canyon below. That was no sweat for Paul. He took his thirty-nine-barrel shotgun and loaded it with crosscut saws and gunpowder. He fired one shot into the upside-down trees, and thirty-nine were sawed off. Babe dragged them all to the mill pond in one trip. This was typical of the conversation at the loggers' table.

At the sawmill, downstream from the logging camp,

the logs were cut into rough or finished lumber. The operation covered several acres, with a large log pond, lumber storage yards, machine shops, bunkhouses, offices and a kitchen and dining room. The sawmill was powered by huge wood-fired steam boilers, since there was no shortage of wood or water.

The men at the sawmill were of a different breed than those at the logging camp. Many were considered part of the community, and their children attended the grammar school. The sawmill provided houses for men with families.

To handle and cut logs up to six feet in diameter and thirty feet long required special equipment and know-how. The key man in the operation was Mr. John Wagner, the millwright. He was Mr. Sawmill. It was his job to keep all the equipment running. Whenever a machine failed, Mr. Wagner was the man of the hour—he worked day and night until the unit was working again.

The number two man in the sawmill was Mr. Ralph Barnes, the head sawyer. He decided how a log should be cut to get the most lumber from it. His decisions had a real influence on the profits of the operation. He stood behind the two spinning six-foot circular saws, one mounted directly above the other with the teeth of the upper saw a quarter of an inch from the teeth of the lower saw. As the large end of the log, fastened on a huge carriage, moved into the two spinning saws, the head sawyer knew from experience how all the cuts were to be made to produce the most profitable yield.

The first cut would be a slab off the side of the log, which fell onto turning rollers, then moved along to other rollers to be carried to another cutting or its final destination. The carriage returned to its original position, the log was turned with the sawed side down, and it returned to the saws as another slab was ripped off. Twice more and the round log was squared off, and could be cut into beams, planks or boards. These moved on spinning rollers to smaller saws for final cutting.

Fresh or "green" lumber was stacked in the yard to cure and dry, then hauled by team and wagon to Sheridan to be sold or shipped by rail. When the local people needed lumber, they bought it directly from the mill and hauled it themselves.

As production improved at the sawmill and demand increased at the sales yard in Sheridan, it was clear that the transportation system from the mill to the Sheridan yard would have to change—team and wagon was too slow. Several alternatives were discussed, including a railroad line and a water flume.

My father campaigned among all the neighbors for the railroad. He took the position that it would be a real benefit to the community, since hay, grain, livestock and other farm products could all be moved by rail, whereas the flume could be used only for lumber. I listened to many arguments and debates at the store. My father refused to let them cross our land with a flume, but he was prepared to give them a free right of way, in fact extra land, for a rail side loading yard.

The lumber company's position was that they had an ample water supply and almost all the materials for the flume construction. The railroad would be much more expensive. My father tried to get the neighbors to stand firm, but he failed, and the flume was built—though not on D.C. Walker's property.

It was eight miles from the sawmill to the sales yard, over variable terrain. The trough had to have an even slope all the way down, which meant that in some areas it was a trench in the ground, while in other places it was high in the air. At Buell the flume was about thirty feet above the ground, and less than a mile away it was seventy five or eighty feet high.

It took more than a year to complete the flume project. When it was finished, some of the water flowing down

The elevated lumber flume near Buell.

Note the split rail fence at the left.

Mill Creek was diverted to the intake of the flume. Men placed the lumber from the mill into the current of water, and in three hours it arrived at the receiving pond in Sheridan. There it was yarded out, stacked, stored, sold or shipped by rail.

For the most part the flume worked well, but there were some problems. Leaks in the trough were common and hard to plug, lumber occasionally jammed up, and water and even lumber poured over the sides sometimes. In winter windstorms, some of the taller sections blew down, and water and lumber poured out, damaging farm land. During cold weather the water spilling over the side would freeze into long icicles, which could be dangerous when they broke off.

To control these problems there was a full time crew of flume walkers who made sure the lumber kept moving. A phone line was installed, and if a problem developed, the flume walker would call back to the lumberyard to stop them from putting more lumber into the trough. Of course, the flume walker was usually at the opposite end of his beat when a jam started. The lumber could back up for great distances, with almost no water coming through to float away the jam. Water behind the jam poured over the sides until the problem was solved.

There were some advantages to living near the flume. Some of the neighbors planted gardens where the flume passed over their land, and tapped it for irrigation. Clarence and I sometimes climbed up to the walkway and waited for a large plank to come along. We hopped on for a ride, then walked back home. Often men from the sawmill rode a plank down to the store, bought what they needed and walked back.

The logging and lumbering operation was important to the Buell area. It employed many men, contributed to the area's economy, and it contributed to the education of the two Walker boys.

Courting

Courting, or sparking as we called it, was pretty restricted in our community. There were not too many ways a young man could meet a gal. At least, there were not many ways her mother would approve, and Mother's approval was important.

A teen-age lad's only transportation was shank's mare, which did not do much for romance, expecially in the winter season. How could a young blade expect his light of love to go for a walk in the rain or in a snowstorm? About his best hope would be to walk with her to and from the schoolhouse occasionally, if the girl happened to live on the same road he did. Even so, there was usually a sister or brother present. If any serious romance started to develop at this age, the lad could depend on the gal's mother stepping in and putting a stop to it.

Things were easier for a fellow over twenty. The swain would have had time to save some money or would have a steady job. He might have a new Sears Roebuck mail-order blue serge suit, and possibly driving horse and buggy. If he took a shine to a pretty miss, and wanted to make a real impression, he might stop at the store before his Sunday afternoon call for one of the two-pound ribbon-decorated fancy boxes of bon-bons. These were not the machine-dipped chocolates that sold for twenty cents per pound. They were super-special hand-dipped chocolates. The two-pound box would set the young man back a buck or more—a full day's wages.

When young Lothario arrived with his present, if the weather was fair, the young lady might suggest they sit on the rocking chairs on the front porch, this being about the extent of the girl's privileges. Of course, there was the ever-present hazard that other members of the family might stroll by at the most inopportune moment, or even decide to plunk down in one of the chairs.

If the weather was bad, they might find a bit of privacy in the parlor, but usually that room was as cold as an icebox and the ventilation was not the greatest. If a fire had been lighted in the parlor stove, it was a good sign that Mother approved of the young man and had no doubts as to his intentions.

The parlor walls were hung with photographs of grandparents, uncles and aunts in oval frames. The expressions on some of their faces were enough to stop a self-winding clock, or chill the ardor of the most aggressive suitor. The couple would sit on the red velour sofa, which had a colorful pillow at each end with painted designs. One was usually a big American Eagle and the other the United States flag. These were prized possessions, won by one of the men in the family at the county fair shooting gallery. The other chairs in the room usually had needlepoint seat covers with designs so pretty you almost hesitated to sit on them.

For her guest's entertainment, the girl might haul out the stereoscope and the dust-covered box of pictures which the family had bought from an itinerant peddler. The next item on the program would be the gal's collection of postcards. At this point Mother would appear with a bowl of fresh popcorn or apples. Then Junior might pop in to show the gentleman guest his new pocketknife, and the young man would begin to wonder if he would ever get anywhere.

For the swain's next call the family picture album

would be featured, and everything was coming up roses.

The picture was a little different if the daughter was heading into her late twenties or thirties and the masculine calls were beginning to dry up. Something had to be done to keep the "old maid ghost" away. The old maid idea was a bitter pill to every mother. The situation had to change or there would be no grandchildren to hold on her knee. So, whenever an eligible male surfaced she would turn on the charm and roll out the red carpet to make the most of the opportunity. Sometimes it worked, but sometimes all this kindness killed the goose that might have laid the golden egg—the suitor smelled a rodent and took off.

In our community there was a surplus of men and a shortage of women, so a gal could be picky and choosy. Even if she were a widow with two uncontrollable brats, or a sphinx who seldom uttered a word, or a compulsive talker who wouldn't let a man get a word in edgewise, or if her specifications across the backside could best be described as wide as a barn door, still she had a chance. The fellow might not be Prince Charming. If he was an oddball bachelor, he usually could stand some polishing, especially if he was a tobacco chewer or if he had broken his razor and had several weeks growth of stubble on his chin. His suit might look as though it had not been exposed to the flatiron within the memory of man. Mother, ever anxious to be helpful, and maybe thinking that a good wife could cure his shortcomings, might whip up a good meal and extend an invitation. Here at the table the gentleman's conversation, manners, and general qualifications might help him win out—or he might run out of invitations to return.

The annual Basket Social fund raiser for the grammar school sometimes gave young people a chance to meet. If a lad had trouble getting his foot in the door, the Basket Social might be his answer. Each girl in the neighborhood would decorate a cardboard box with fancy colored paper, ribbons, or paper flowers and fill it with sandwiches, cake, pie and other goodies, and include her name inside the box. The boxes were auctioned off, and the fellow who bought the basket ate supper with the gal who made it.

The night of the big show all the baskets were displayed on a large table at the grammar school. This event always brought out a big crowd. None of the men were supposed to know which basket belonged to any particular girl, but sometimes there were leaks, and when a certain basket came up for auction, there would be more than the usual interest from some of the bidders. These rivalries ran up the price of the baskets and built up the school coffers.

One of these basket socials followed my eighth grade grammar school graduation. I was interested in an attractive girl in my class, Reva Merrick, but it was a one-way street—Reva never showed any interest in me. Reva's family lived just up the road from the Ridgeways, who had a daughter Kate, and a son Dale. Dale was quite a young blade in the community because he owned a new rubber tire buggy and a driving horse. Kate and Reva were great friends, and for this particular basket social, they decided to make their baskets almost exactly alike.

On the evening of the social, their two baskets were on the table—one had a colored rose on the top and the other had the same kind of rose on the side. I had no idea which one was Reva's and which was Kate's. When the entertainment was over and the auction began, I started getting nervous. I was not packing very much of this world's gold. I had a buck seventy-five, and I knew that any competition might wipe me out of the running.

The call came for an auctioneer and Dale Ridgeway stepped up on the stage. Soon the first basket was offered and the bidding was rapid. . .it reached one dollar and then slowed. . .Dale called out,"One dollar once, twice, last call! Sold for one dollar! Next basket please!" The bids were coming fast and baskets were going for as much as two dollars. Considering that two dollars was more than a man made for twelve hours' work, those were top prices.

Finally the two identical baskets came up for sale. Here I was, all sixteen years of me, decked out in a new mail-order blue serge suit, and I faced a problem. I had a strong yen for Reva's basket, but I had absolutely no information. It was a tense moment and I was beginning to sweat, when suddenly Reva walked over to where I was standing and whispered, "My basket has the rose on top."

Never until that moment did I know what my rating was with Reva or that she wanted me to have her basket. Although my finances were on the lightweight side, it was my time to act, and I was ready. Soon the basket with the rose on top was in the auctioneer's hands, and I bid fifty cents. That alerted Skinny Jones, another lad in my class who had an eye on Reva. He figured I had inside information, so he blurted out "Sixty cents!" We were in a bidding contest, making ten to fifteen cent jumps. My bid was up to one buck sixty-five and I was hoping against hope that Skinny would run out of funds, when auctioneer Dale barked, "I bid five dollars!" That did me in. I was folded—crushed, and so was Skinny. Kate's brother ate the basket social supper with Reva and on the following Sunday afternoon, who do you think I saw driving by the country store with Reva in a new rubber-tire buggy? I did not own even a bicycle, and never again did I recover my former rating with Reva. With all Dale's clout, Reva gave me the mitten.

At that point I was graduated out of more than the Buell grammar school. I always had a strong suspicion that Kate Ridgeway had tipped off her brother about Reva's basket. In the fall Reva went away to a high school in Sheridan and every Friday evening Dale went to pick Reva up and bring her home, then on Sunday evening he took her back to the place where she lived in town. They were married the following summer. That was my last Basket Social fling.

A fellow who was not lucky at socials and couldn't get introduced to a gal at a dance still had one more chance. Late August and early September every year was hop-picking time. Folks gathered at the hopyards from many areas. The hops, like spongy pine cones, grew in clusters on the vines and were stripped or picked off by hand. Pickers would move down the rows in pairs, one on each side of the row, picking hops into four-and-a-half-bushel baskets. Two full baskets were called a "box" of hops. When the pickers had two full baskets, they would call out "Hop check!" and the foreman and assistant would dump the hops into a burlap bag and give the pickers a small numbered card, value fifty cents, legal tender at the store.

This was an ideal set-up for the eager beaver who wanted a little conversation with the girl who was the apple of his eye. All he had to do was casually stroll around and pause for a few moments of visiting where the gal was picking hops with her Aunt Matilda. Aunty was a little more broad-minded than usual if he started picking hops into the young lady's basket—it was the same as money in the bank.

If the visitor was a lonesome bachelor trying to crash the gate with one of the older fems, the strategy worked just as well, and always provided conversation. At least the fellow could get to first base, and after that let the chips fall where they may.

Often an acquaintance started this way might blossom around the campfire in the evening. Here everyone got a chance to show off their talents singing, playing an instrument or telling stories, and there was always plenty of conversation. This might give Cupid just the chance he needed.

Once a fellow decided he had found the girl of his

dreams, he would make his sales pitch. If and when the gal finally said "Yes," he still had one more wide river to cross. It was the custom of the time for the suitor to ask the lady's father for permission to marry her. Sometimes this was a rough order, but it was the way things were done and it was the young man's move. Of course, by the time he had been through the long courtship under Mother's eagle eye, there was little doubt of his reception. When he was a hit with his future mother-in-law, she took every opportunity to tell her neighbors all about it.

Now it was the young woman's time to buttonhole her friends and brag about her wonderful fiance, her future happiness, and so forth. When her friends came to visit, she pulled out her cedar hope chest, filled with crocheted doilies, handkerchiefs, trims for pillow slips, linens and patchwork quilts. When she married, the hope chest and a few personal items went with her.

The wedding might be a grand spread or a modest affair, depending on the family's economic situation at the time. After the ceremony the lovebirds took off with horse and buggy for parts unknown. A few days later, the horse and buggy returned with the weary newly-weds, and they moved into their new home.

A group of the couple's friends might decide to give them a wedding reception they would not forget, a shivaree. They would gather outside the house in the middle of the night, and at the signal, bedlam would break out. They rang cow bells, banged tin pans, blasted horns, and generally made as much noise as possible. Then the shouting would start, calling the bride and groom to come out. . .wake up. . .let us in!

Finally a lamp beamed through a window. The door opened and there stood the bride and groom to receive their unexpected guests. The blushing bride had to make coffee and endure plenty of wise cracks and jokes until at last the gang took pity on them and left, with lots of handshaking and best wishes for happiness. A shivaree in the community was something the couple long remembered, and provided plenty of neighborhood conversation.

In spite of all the obstacles, Cupid was always on the job.

Book Learning

It was on a Monday morning in September, 1905, that Mother put away the five-pound lard pail that Clarence had used to carry his lunch to school. She replaced it with a 10-pound lard pail because there would be two lunches to carry—George was about to start his book learning.

There were many families in our neighborhood with five or six children, and the Buell grammar school had two class rooms with thirty-five or more students. The schoolmaster taught the older children in the fifth through eighth grades, and an assistant teacher taught the primer through fourth grades. The instructors were carefully selected by the school board. They were models of propriety and they had the support of the people in the community.

Five days each week school would begin at 9:00 am with all the students standing at their desks reciting the Pledge of Allegiance to the Flag or singing patriotic songs. At the front of the room, next to the teacher's desk, there was a long recitation bench. The instructor would call up one class at a time to the bench and teach the lesson while the other students in the room worked on their various assignments.

Each student's desk had an inkwell at the upper edge with a hinged metal cover, and a space below the top for

My primer copybook — learning the art of writing, 1905.

school books. Almost every student had a slate for writing or figuring that could be wiped clean with a cloth after each use.

For my first term, I had a primer book for reading and a copy book with a series of pictures across the top of each page. Each picture had its name written below, and our job was to copy the writing. We learned mostly by rote memorization and repetition.

For the primer class lessons there was a large wall chart with pictures and words on each page. The students would pronounce the word and spell out the letters aloud, then the teacher turned to the next page. When the lesson was over, the teacher had the students return to their desks, and called up the next class.

There was no running water in the school building. Drinking water was from a hand pump in the school yard. Girls had their own drinking cups, most boys cupped their hands to drink. The other facilities were two small square buildings a considerable distance back of the school building. If a student wanted to leave the class, the rule was to hold up one finger for a drink of water, two for a nature call, and the teacher would nod permission to go. Girls were generally too shy to leave the class—they would wait until recess, and even then a girl would not go alone. She would always get another girl to walk with her, in the interest of modesty.

The primer grade was a six-month term, and at the end of each month the teacher handed us our report cards indicating days absent, times late, deportment, application and our grades. The report card had to have a parent's signature, and who wanted to face Father or Mother with a lousy grade? It was an incentive to work hard.

The school had rules, and if they were violated there were penalties. It was not uncommon to see the schoolmaster or the teacher rap a student's open hand with a ruler. The teacher had the support of the parents

My seventh grade class — the teacher was Lucy Kopan.

Buell, Ore. Public School

6th Grade 1st Division

	1st Mo.	2nd Mo.	3d Mo.	4th Mo.	5th Mo.	6th Mo.	7th Mo.	8th Mo.	9th Mo.	10th Mo.	R
Days Present	21	19	15	17	15	20	20	19			
Days Absent	0	0	0	0	0	0	0	7			
Times Late	0	0	0	0	0	0	0	0			
Deportment	100	100	95	90	98	99	100	100			
Application	100	100	100	[illegible]	100	100	100	100			
	S	S	S	S	S	S	S	S	S	S	R
Reading	90	93	95	96	97	98	[illegible]	95			
Writing	75	76	77	78	80	82	84	82			
Spelling	92	88	96	98	100	90	100	85			
Arithmetic	48	48	82	88	76	100	75	78			
Geography	97	90	95	96	94	95	95	95			
Language	85	98	70	75	[illegible]	100		84			
Physiology	75	76	[illegible]	78	[illegible]	80		78			
History	95	90	C	C	C	C	C	92			
Civil Gov'mt.											

Your final in Arith would not promote you, but your general average does. —

My report card, 1912

and the community when it came to discipline.

I recall a few times when I ran afoul of the discipline policies at the school. Helen Fletcher, a red-headed girl in my third-grade class, sat at the desk behind mine. One day the teacher asked Helen to come to her desk, and as Helen was getting up I put one foot in her path. Down she went in the aisle, her skirt askew. Several of the children laughed, and to say that that redhead was mad would be putting it mildly. I was suddenly very studious, with my nose in my geography book, but it did no good—both Helen and the teacher knew what had happened.

The teacher gave me a personally conducted tour of the blackboard. In front of the whole schoolroom she told me to stand and write fifty times, "I tripped Helen and I am very sorry." I wrote and wrote while the teacher conducted her classes. From time to time the teacher would glance over or make a count and tell me to keep writing. Finally, when I had nearly covered the blackboard, she counted fifty and I returned to my desk. That was the last stunt I pulled for some time.

One warm spring day, however, while I was eating my noon repast of a boiled egg, bread and butter and an apple, a classmate, Willie Bennett, sat down next to me. We both developed a case of spring fever and he suggested we play hooky for the afternoon and go wading in Mill Creek. We took off, and when the bell tolled at one o'clock we were in the creek.

Everything was going great until Mr. Sweeney, a rancher in the neighborhood, came along on his way to the country store. He didn't say anything to us, but when I got home at four o'clock, my explanations got a bad reception. I found it very uncomfortable to sit down anywhere for the rest of that day, and when I got to school the next morning, the teacher asked that I stay after school. Willie got the same invitation, and we both did our share of worrying all day. We got a real tongue-lashing that afternoon—no more hooky for me!

Clarence was a year ahead of me in school, and since he was one of the larger boys in his class, he landed the job of school janitor. In the winter season, he arrived half an hour early every morning to fire up the stove in each classroom and bank it with wood so that the room would be comfortable by school time. At recess and at lunch he would refuel the stoves, then again at about 2:30. The stoves stood at the center of each classroom, and each had a metal shield to circulate the warm air through the room. After school let out at four, Clarence would sweep both classrooms and police up the place. He did this five days a week for the school term, and his compensation was a buck fifty a week. He held on to this gravy-train job until his eighth grade graduation in 1913, then I latched on to it until I graduated the next year.

Athletics at our school were rather limited, especially in the rainy season. There was only one game that we could play in the wet months, a modified form of hockey called shinney. The players used an oak stick for the club and a tin can for the puck. It was a rough game when those oak sticks started swinging, and you had better not get in front of that flying tin can. Sometimes feuds developed and if the teacher had to restore order, shinney was off-limits for a few days.

When the ground dried out baseball was our game. We had no factory-made equipment—we produced our own ball and bat. For the ball I would unravel the string from a discarded pair of cotton work socks and wind it tightly into a ball. I made two paper patterns to fit the ball, then cut two ball covers from a discarded pair of Mother's high laced shoes and sewed them onto the ball. For the bat we went into the woods to select a small ash tree, and whittled it with a jack-knife to the size and shape we wanted. We had to make do with materials at hand.

The last day of each school year was always a red-letter day. All the students were polished up, and there were picnic tables set up in the school yard. Classes started at nine, and about 10:30 parents began arriving with all kinds of food and goodies. School let out at 11:30 and soon everyone was talking and visiting. The tables were groaning with the special dishes and everyone ate until they could eat no more.

At these picnics the schoolmarm had a chance to mingle with parents and others from the community. At the time, it seemed there was always a shortage of eligible young women and a surplus of men. The schoolmarm was usually a recent graduate of a teacher's college, and came from another town. She was earning a salary and was always well-groomed and carefully dressed—it would not be too long before one of the local eligibles had his eye on her. Of course, she had agreed to the school term, and had to be most circumspect in her behavior, but often at the end of the term the school board was looking up the county school superintendent to get a new teacher.

A grammar school education was thought to be enough for many people at the time—after that they could rely on practical experience. Of all the students graduating from the Buell grammar school, only a few went to high school, and only two that we knew went on to college. Often a college student was considered an educated fool—life in a rural area did not demand a college education.

Our parents wanted Clarence and me to go on with our schooling, though. When Clarence graduated he spent a year at the Dallas Academy, a substitute for high school. Dallas was twelve miles from Buell, and Clarence walked home every Friday afternoon and walked back to Dallas the following Sunday. To help pay the expense he took a job as a night clerk in one of the leading hotels.

The next fall our parents wanted us to go to high school together. The nearest school was at Salt Creek, four miles from Buell. In the morning, the walk to school was no problem, especially down the long grade of Butler Hill. The return hike uphill was something else—it called for several rest stops along the way. This was O.K. until the winter set in with rain, snow and sleet turning the road into mud. For a while we rode our horses, but then we had another problem—where to leave them during the day. Finally we arranged with a farmer half a mile from the high school to stable them while we were in school.

At that time the game of basketball was becoming popular, and Salt Creek High was not going to be out of date. The people in the community contributed money, labor and materials to build a gymnasium. It was not exactly the last word in gymnasiums, but it had four walls at least three-fourths of the way to the eaves of the roof, with the open space covered with chicken wire netting—plenty of fresh air on wintry days. The floor was dirt.

By dragging in almost all the boys in the school, a team was organized. Clarence, being a six-footer, had no trouble landing the center position. Being a lightweight, about the only position I could expect was in the cheering section.

The Salt Creek team played all the neighboring high school teams, and soon were the champions. They flung a challenge to the Willamina High School team, nine miles away, who were champs in their area. A Friday night was set for the game. The country store was on the way, five miles from Willamina, so some of the players gathered there after supper on the big game night.

At our house we had a watchdog called Paddy, and a small mongrel named Fritz who had come in from somewhere and decided this was his home. Fritz was a sharpie, and his only purpose in life, as far as I could tell, was to be my playmate or to keep meat from spoiling. Usually I didn't mind when he followed me around, but on this particular evening I was going with the team and did not want him along. We were about three miles along the road to Willamina when who should show up but Fritz. I tried to send him back home. It was a good idea but it didn't work. Finally Clarence said, "Let him come along, he won't be any problem." During the game Fritz stuck close to me.

The game was a tough one but Salt Creek won and after it was over, the team went to an ice cream parlor to celebrate with a soda or dish of ice cream. Fritz, as usual, was center stage, pouring on the charm. A man at the next table noticed Fritz and started playing with him, and soon asked who owned him. Apparently he wanted a dog for his children, and Fritz met his specifications. The man wanted to buy Fritz, and, although I was mad at him for coming, I was not mad enough to want to get rid of him. The man kept playing with Fritz and offered two dollars—a sizable sum, especially for a mongrel dog.

I did not know what to do, and finally asked Clarence. He was no help—he just pointed out that we still had Paddy, and one dog should be enough. It was up to me. I was far from affluent, and I had uses for the two bucks, so I agreed. The man forked over two silver dollars, then got a piece of cord from the store and took off with Fritz.

On the way home some of the boys razzed me about selling Fritz. Of course, it would not have been their problem to carry him for an hour and a half or more on a bareback horse. I had mixed emotions, but a sale was a sale and there was no turning back. We got home late and hit the sack, because there were chores to be done early in the morning.

When we got up in the morning and opened the kitchen door to go to the barn, who was there to say "Good morning?" Fritz, nobody else! I had made a good "sale"—two bucks and I still had Fritz!

We got to school on horseback until about mid-December, when the days grew shorter, the storms were worse and the mud deeper. It was getting rough on us as well as on the horses, and there was the risk of the animals developing mud fever, which our parents did not need. Clarence and I decided to find living quarters in the Salt Creek area for the winter. After some inquiries and scouting, we spotted a hop picker's shack at Ezra Hart's hop yard about three-quarters of a mile from the school. Mr. Hart gave us permission to move in.

It was not luxurious winter quarters, but it would have to do. After all, it had a wood floor, four walls and a roof, and it was near the creek for a supply of water. There was a small stove, a sway-back bed with a straw mattress, two dilapidated chairs and a small table. There were no windows, but you can't have everything.

The firebox of the stove was so small it was almost impossible to generate any heat. It required constant stoking with wood we chopped from nearby trees on the creek bank. It was here we did our studying, cooking, eating and sleeping. Sometimes our food supply would be on the short side before Friday afternoon, so I supplemented our provisions with trout from Salt Creek. This was our fraternity house from Sunday evening to Friday afternoon.

On Fridays after school we treked home through storms and mud to a bath, a change of underwear, clean clothes and Mother's good cooking. She always had something special for us, and after five days of cooking for ourselves, I can assure you she heard no gripes from Clarence or me. On Sunday afternoons we assembled the next week's provisions, some clean towels and other supplies, and packed them on our backs through the mud to our fraternity quarters. We immediately fired up the stove to take off the chill, lit the coal oil lamp, got some supper and turned our attention to Monday's school assignment.

This arrangement prevailed until early May when the weather moderated. Then we packed our worldly belongings and closed our shack for the season. Until the school term ended we went back to riding the horses to school.

All this seemed like a lot of trouble just to go to school, but Mother and Father knew our education was important, and would not hear of our leaving school to work. Looking back now, of course, I realize that they were right.

Clarence and me at our "fraternity house."

Palouse Country

According to the fellows warming the nail kegs and cracker boxes at the country store, the Palouse country of eastern Washington was where the big money was. The wheat farmers there paid the highest wages during the harvest season in late summer. I had sharp ears when the conversation ran on this topic, because, at sixteen, I needed money for high school books and clothes.

That word "Palouse" fascinated me, and I had experience in harvest work, so why shouldn't I try for some of those big wages? But talking about going to eastern Washington when I had never been far from Mother's apron strings was about the same as suggesting a trip to Nepal or Tibet. I buttonholed one of the men who had been talking about Palouse country. From him I learned that there was a Columbia River freight boat that ran between Portland and The Dalles. If I could get a job handling freight on that boat I would be about seventy-five miles closer to the wheat country. The next problem was convincing my parents.

I thought I had better get Clarence's opinion. He said I should go and get in on that big money. He would have liked to come with me, but he had promised to work for some of the neighbors, and besides, one of us should be around to help with the chores at home. His support was all I needed.

The Palouse country bug was really chewing on me, and early in July I presented my plan. My parents didn't take on the idea with open arms, but there was not too much static, so I decided to use the soft-sell method and come back with the idea in a couple days. Finally Father consented, but made it clear that I would be on my own. This was no obstacle, because I always avoided asking my parents for money. If I needed something, I took pride in paying for it. Besides, Mother always told me that "Where there's a will, there's a way."

Father was planning to go into Sheridan for freight the following Monday, and he offered to take me to the depot, so I had to get organized. I had a bed roll of worn blankets and a tarpaulin, a frayed reed suitcase with a leather strap to hold it together, work clothes and $23 in working capital. I packed my blue serge suit, an extra shirt and underclothes, and Mother came forth with a miniature sewing kit that she said I might need. She also handed me five penny-postcards and told me to be sure to write home about my progress and let them know when I would return.

Monday morning I did my share of the chores and outfitted myself in my slightly worn blue jeans, cambric shirt, jumper coat, a new pair of elk hide shoes, and my wide-brim felt hat. Soon we were on the way to Sheridan. We had plenty of conversation, but Father raised no objections to my plan. As I got on the train, he told me to write if I needed money. I thanked him, but had no intention of taking him up on his offer.

The Portland train was a combination of passenger and freight cars, and stopped along the way to pick up some of each. We arived in Portland in the early afternoon, and I walked to the freight docks on the river. The Bailey-Gazert freight boat was loading at the dock to be ready to leave at five the next morning. I called on the captain and asked him to take me on. He asked about my plans and quizzed me about where I came from, but finally agreed to let me work with the crew. He couldn't pay me any wages, but I would get meals, a place to park the carcass for the night, and seventy-five miles of free transportation, so who was I to kick a gift horse in the face? I quickly accepted his offer.

The boat was a steam-powered stern wheeler, and had a crew of three freight handlers, an engineer, and a cook. The captain introduced me to the cook, whose name was Elroy Stevens. The first thing he said to me was "Call me Spike." Apparently he didn't want to be called Elroy, and I guess I don't blame him. Then the captain took me to meet the crew. They were a bit on the rough side—not exactly the type you would pick to marry your favorite daughter.

The captain showed me where I would sleep on the deck. It was not the bridal suite at a fancy hotel, but it served my purpose. For the rest of the afternoon I worked with the crew loading canned goods, sacks of flour and salt, kegs of nails, furniture, and almost any goods or supplies people up the river might need. When the bell tolled for supper, I shared the crew's dinner, which was excellent. Spike Stevens knew that the captain depended on the cook to keep his crew satisfied. If the food was bad, a mutiny was in the making. A while later I spread out my bed roll and turned in. The next thing I knew the whistle was blasting at four in the morning, time to hit the deck and eat breakfast, with no lack of appetite on my part. When breakfast was over the whistle blew and the Bailey-Gazert pulled away from the dock. We were on our way!

We steamed twelve miles down the Willamette River to where it joined the Columbia, then started upstream toward The Dalles. Our first port of call was Camas, Washington, and then we moved on to Washougal. At both stops we unloaded our sacks and boxes and took on sacks of grain, bales of hay, cans of cream and other items to be delivered at The Dalles. Freight boats like the

Bailey-Gazert carried supplies of all kinds for merchants, farmers and ranchers all along the Columbia, and brought farm products back to town. The river boats were an important form of transportation, more economical than team and wagons.

The Columbia is the second largest river in the United States and is one of the most scenic of all rivers. It cuts through the Cascade mountains beyond Washougal, and the river has carved a gorge that is something to see. To look up from the middle of the river at these mountains on both sides, at the towering rocks and green timber, with waterfalls flowing into the river—it was an experience. Many people travel long distances and spend sizeable sums of money to see the Columbia Gorge, and here I was getting it all free.

Steaming slowly upstream, struggling against the current, there was plenty of time for the crew to sit around on the freight and talk. They told me about the river, the towns we were passing through, and they even gave me pointers on where to get harvest work.

Old Spike Stevens was a student of nature and Oregon history. He took special care to tell me about the points of interest. He explained about The Dalles—I thought the name was unusual. He said the French Canadian Fur Company employees had named the town, and that "dalles" meant narrow water or rapids. The Columbia is so narrow and flows so fast at that point that the Lewis and Clark expedition had been forced to portage around the rapids there to continue their trip to the Pacific.

After we passed through the gorge our next stop was the town of Hood River, where we unloaded more cargo and picked up cans of cream. Soon after dinner we crossed the river and unloaded freight at Lyle, Washington. From there to The Dalles it was smooth sailing.

I learned from the crew that it was too early in the season to go to Palouse country for grain harvesting, but men were being hired at Arlington, Oregon to work harvesting alfalfa hay. When we pulled in to The Dalles that evening, I bid my shipmates goodbye and headed for the train station.

Sitting at the Union Pacific depot all alone, with my ticket in hand, I began to wonder if this was such a good idea, but finally I heard the train whistle and soon I was on the cushions.

The train arrived in Arlington early in the morning. As in other farming areas, there was a place near the railroad depot called the "slave market" where itinerant men looking for work would collect. The men on the boat had told me that farmers and ranchers who needed hired hands came here. I headed for the slave market with my frayed reed suitcase and bed roll. While waiting I looked over the other men there—they were some rough-looking characters. Some of their clothes looked as if they had not been exposed to soap and water for a long time. Some of these men were diamonds in the rough, however. When you knew them better you discovered they were kind, generous and always ready to lend a hand. From my experience at the country store I was familiar with the type.

After I had waited a short while, a hay rancher from Willow Creek arrived at the slave market. He wanted a man to operate a mowing machine to cut his alfalfa hay and would pay three dollars a day, plus board and keep. This was the deal for me—I bounced over to him and offered my services, giving him a soft-sell sales pitch. He asked a few questions and soon we were in his Model T Ford on the way to Willow Creek. He had a sizable operation, and I ended up working for him nearly a month.

For that month, I was up each day at 5:30 to water, feed and harness the horses. Then we had breakfast and were in the field mowing alfalfa by seven. I piloted a team of horses hitched to a mowing machine with an eight-foot sickle bar. Don't ask me why the seat of a mowing machine has to be cast iron, but let me tell you that a ten-hour day spent bouncing over the alfalfa fields on one can be painful. I won't elaborate—it might be embarassing. Other men raked and stacked the hay after it was cut. This was the routine six days a week, and on Sunday I went swimming and washed my clothes in Willow Creek. When the mowing was finished, the rancher handed me seventy-eight dollars in cash—the most money I had ever earned in my life on one job.

The rancher drove me back into Arlington and soon I was back on the Union Pacific train, arriving in Colfax, Washington in the Palouse country early in the morning. Again, I went to the slave market and joined the characters there. The wheat harvest was in full swing and it was not long before a wheat farmer came around to hire a man as a header-wagon driver, offering four dollars a day. This was a windfall, and I jumped at the chance.

This Palouse country was a new world for me, all vast rolling hills for miles and miles, with roads in the canyons or at the base of hills. This was the heart of the wheat-growing area, the Bread Basket of the West, and the ranches were enormous. Ranchers didn't talk about acreage, they talked sections of wheat. A section is 640 acres and many of the ranchers farmed several sections.

This was a "dry farming" area—they prepared the land in the late summer or early fall, then seeded it. When the winter snow melted in the spring, the moisture germinated the wheat. Because there was so little rainfall in that area, the stalks of grain grew only six or eight inches high when the heads of wheat matured. To harvest these low wheat heads they used a special head-cutting machine and a specially constructed wagon bed to haul the wheat heads to the grain separator. The header cutting machine was powered by six or eight mules. The header wagon was built to harvest grain from the steep sides of the rolling hills. The front wheels were about six feet apart, but the rear wheels were about double the normal distance apart. This extra width at the rear of the wagon gave it stability on the slopes where an ordinary wagon would tip over. The wagon bed was constructed of tongue-and-groove flooring lumber to prevent shelled wheat from being lost through the cracks. One side of the wagon bed had a three-foot wall, and there was no wall on the other side. At each end of the wagon bed, the wall tapered from the three foot edge to the floor level. I had to drive the wagon with the high wall toward the lower side of the hill, to keep the load from sliding off the wagon.

The wagon had no seat—the driver stood at the front of the wagon bed clutching a post called a Jacob's staff to keep from sliding off. Keeping your balance was a trick while the wagon wheels rolled along on a steep slope with slippery wheat chaff underfoot. You also had to keep the four mules headed in the right direction over and around the curves of the hills. The idea was to keep the wagon bed under the elevated chute of the header cutter machine. If the wagon was not under the end of the chute the wheat fell to the ground and there would be a yell from the machine operator. Too many yells and the driver was not around any more—there would be a new face to pilot the four pairs of long-ears. Being four hundred miles from home I was not looking for trouble, so who was I to talk back to the header machine operator?

When the wagon bed was loaded the driver pulled away to deliver the load to the threshing machine. Another header wagon would pull in behind and start loading. Sometimes there were six or more header wagons, depending on the size of the operation.

The header wagon driver's day started at four in the morning when the threshing machine steam whistle blew. I had to get up, water the four hayburners, toss them a bundle of nourishment, throw the harness on each one, and dash to the cookshack. A splash with soap and cold water would remove a few layers of accumulation, and I was headed for the table, which would be groaning under the load of good food. After cramming down every bite I could possibly hold I would dash back to the mules, hitch them up to the header wagon and drive to the field, to be ready to load by six. To be late on the job was an almost unforgivable sin.

By ten my stomach thought my throat had been cut, but there was no coffee break—only more mule skinning and loading and unloading wheat heads. I was sure noon would never, never come, but finally the whistle blew, and I would unhitch, water and feed the mules and head for the cookhouse. It was on this job that I learned how loudly my stomach could growl—a man would say "I'm as hungry as a bitch wolf with fifteen pups." I don't know the details about the wolf, but this sixteen-year-old could eat and eat until I could not stuff another morsel down the gullet, and still be hungry. A wheat rancher had to put on a good spread at mealtime, or he would lose his hired help.

After dinner it was back to the mule routine, and into the fields by one. The hours between one and seven in the wheat fields always seemed like the longest stretch of time I ever endured. There was nothing but a jug of water cooled by the 100-degree sunshine to keep you from almost dying of thirst. I was sure that starvation would do me in, but somehow I managed to hold on until the last whistle blast. Then again it was the mule and cookshack routine, and at 8:30 I would spread my tarpaulin in the stubble field with the sky for a roof and lay out my bedroll. No sleeping pills required!

It was rough and rugged, but I was earning more than I ever had before, and I wasn't bellyaching. Then one night, some time after midnight, I woke up to gentle rain drops that soon developed into a steady downpour in the pitch dark. It was my move, but where? My bedding was still dry thanks to the canvas tarpaulin, but my clothes were not in the bed and they were soaked. I thought of the header wagon with its matched lumber floor—it would be dry underneath. I grabbed my clothes and bedding and headed for the wagon in the dark.

The mules tied to the side of the wagon were trying to turn their rears to the storm, but their tethers were too short and they couldn't get turned. Frustrated, they stomped, twisted, and thrashed a deep mud hole under their feet. I was wet and cold and wide awake all night.

When daylight finally came I pulled on my wet clothes, but one shoe was missing. I remembered bringing both shoes under the wagon, but I looked and looked and no shoe. Finally I caught sight of a small black metal object under one of the mules' front feet. It dawned on me that that was probably the end of one of my shoelaces. The mule was standing on my shoe in six inches of mud. Crawling out from under the wagon, I moved the mule and excavated my shoe from the mud puddle by pulling on the lace. I scooped out the mud with my hands, but pulling that shoe on over my wet sock...in the semi-darkness at 4:00 in the morning...I was miserable.

Fortunately, it was not long until breakfast. The crew members reported a variety of experiences of the night, but none of them could beat mine. The fields were too wet for threshing, so several of the men planned to go into Colfax for the day. About this time, it seemed to me that my career as a header wagon driver did not hold too much charm, so I went to the boss and asked for my dough. He wrote me a check for twenty dollars for the five days I had worked, and I gathered up my bedroll and frayed suitcase, and we headed for Colfax.

My working capital had now reached the huge sum of ninety-eight dollars. That was not a bad showing for a sixteen-year-old's efforts. On the ride into town, one of the men mentioned that a freight boat would be leaving from Colfax for The Dalles that evening. This information was music to my ears, and, with 98 sheckels, plus $10.75 of my original capital, I was really on Cloud Nine.

When we reached Colfax, I thought I had better hold a conference with myself. First, I could stand a bit of sharpening up, so I walked into a barber shop to start the program. I cashed my twenty-dollar check and paid for the haircut, then asked the barber if I could park my suitcase and bedroll there while I finished up my errands. The next item on my agenda was to go to the post office and buy a money order for $98 and mail it to my parents, and let them know my plans. Putting that money in the mail made me feel mighty proud. My next stop was the freight boat office to interview the captain of the boat.

The captain told me that the water in the Palouse River was so low in the hot summer weather that they had been forced to suspend operations the week before. At this point, Cloud Nine fell out of the sky for me—I only had $10.40 left to my name.

With the boat out of commission, the railroad was the only means of transportation. I took off for the ticket office to check out the prices. It was twelve dollars to Portland—forget that. The fare to Hood River, halfway between Portland and The Dalles was $10.60—still over my limit. The man in the office told me that a ticket to The Dalles was $7.70, and that settled the matter. I said, "One ticket, please." The train would leave that evening.

I had time on my hands, so I strolled the streets of Colfax, wondering if sending the 98 to my father had been such a hot idea. It was done, though, and I recalled my agreement that I was on my own. I decided to find a solution at The Dalles.

Gazing in a bakery window, I realized that the habit of eating was still with me. The cinnamon rolls sure had a strong appeal. I took on a dozen for an investment of twenty-five cents, which carried me along until about five o'clock, when I went back for another dozen. That dozen would have to see me through to The Dalles.

In the meantime, I gave some thought to the possibilities of employment at The Dalles, and I realized that the mail-order blue serge in the suitcase had undergone some hardships and might need some freshening up. I took them to the nearest clothes pressing place. The presser man apparently sensed my situation, because for fifty cents he performed a remarkable feat of removing dust and packing wrinkles from my blue serge, necktie, and cambric workshirt, which I had washed in Willow Creek when I left the fields. There was a small room at the back of the presser's shop where a man could wait in his drawers or in the raw while he was having his only suit pressed. My elk-hide work shoes looked rather rough, especially the one that had undergone the mud ordeal, so I went next door to a shoeshine place to improve their looks for another fifteen-cent investment. I did not look exactly like I had just walked out of a fashionable men's clothing store, but at least I was presentable.

At 8:30 I boarded the train to dine on my remaining cinnamon rolls and wear out the night on the cushions. By the time we arrived at The Dalles in the morning the cinnamon rolls had long since burned out, so I asked a brakeman at the station where I could get a low-cost breakfast. He directed me to a nearby fry-cook place operated by a Chinaman. The menu board on the wall indicated ham and eggs for twenty-five cents, so I splurged.

Walking back to the depot, I noticed The Dalles Hotel across the street. I left my frayed suitcase and bedroll with the bellhop, to be picked up later. Now my cash reserves were down to $1.30 and I was still 150 miles from free bed and board.

It was a warm, sunny morning and as it was my first chance to see the town, I decided to take a walk up the main street and look the situation over. I must admit, I wondered what the day would hold. It was too early for the stores to be open, so I walked along looking in the windows. In the window of Rice-McCoy's Men's Furnishings there was a small sign, "Salesmen Wanted." I parked myself in the entry way directly in front of the glass door and waited for the store to open. In a few minutes a man stopped and stood behind me, and soon two more men joined the line-up, all neatly dressed, presenting a first-rate appearance. I realized that in spite of the best efforts of the clothes presser and the shoeshine man, I could not compete with these fashion-plates.

It was important that I land the job—the pressure was on yours truly. Soon a well-dressed man walked past the line-up, turned the key in the door and told us he would be with us shortly. I was thinking fast to come up with something to catch the man's eye, and I recalled the stunt I had learned at the country store—a fast way to wrap and tie a package and snap the twine with my fingers. It was an attention-getter at the store—maybe it would work here.

Soon the gentleman opened the door and asked me to step in. We walked to the counter at the rear of the store. The man introduced himself as Mr. Halley Rice, who owned the store with Mr. McCoy. Mr. Rice had just received his "Greetings" notice from the U.S. Army to report for service in the war in Europe. They had decided to hold a closing-out sale, so they needed some extra sales help.

Mr. Rice was very courteous, asking where I had been working, how I happened to be in The Dalles, and so on. I replied briefly, then he asked if I had ever worked in a store or had sales experience. I replied, "Mr. Rice, would you please hand me a box of those shoes behind you on the shelf?" My approach seemed to amuse him, and he handed me the box of shoes.

Without a word I reached up to the roll of wrapping

paper above the counter, pulled out and cut off the proper length of paper, laid it on the counter and centered the box on the paper. In a few moves I had wrapped, tied, and cut the twine with my fingers, and I handed the wrapped box to him. He looked it over, smiled and said, "You're hired." He inquired as to the pay I would expect, and I replied, "Mr. Rice, I will leave that in your hands. You pay me what you think I am worth."

When he found that I needed room and board he told me about a Mrs. Callaghan who operated a boarding house, and he called her for me. I went back to the hotel for my baggage and walked to Mrs. Callaghan's. She assigned me the first bedroom that I had been exposed to for more than a month. I took a shower, ate a meal, and returned to the store, which was to open for the sale that afternoon. Mr. Rice furnished me new shoes, shirt, tie, and so on. Now I was ready.

During the sale, the store opened at eight each morning and closed at nine every evening. When Mr. Rice totaled the sales for each clerk at the end of the day I was always either number one or near the top. The sale was to end on Saturday, so I wrote to my parents that I would be in Sheridan the following Monday, and meet Father at the livery stable when he came into Sheridan for supplies.

The store closed the night of the ninth day of the sale. When I returned the following morning, Mr. Rice expressed appreciation for my work and made me a present of the clothing he had furnished. Then he gave me a check for $31.50, or $3.50 per day. This had surely been a gravy-train ride of a job compared to the header wagon workout. I paid Mrs. Callaghan for my board and keep and set off with my worldly posessions for the railroad station. Soon I was on the train cushions enroute home.

My stock was at a new high—I had coin in my pocket, new clothes, and I would soon be back in Buell. When I reached the Sheridan livery stable, Father and Clarence were waiting. We gathered up the supplies for the country store and were on our way home.

Final Buell

Late in the summer of 1915, our parents made a difficult decision. Clarence and I were enrolled in a high school four miles away, and our parents decided that it was too much for us to walk back and forth every day in all kinds of weather. They sold the store and farm that we had built from nothing into a successful operation. With a team and wagon we moved our belongings the twenty miles to Monmouth.

At this point the Buell saga draws to a close. It was more than sixty years later that I visited Buell again. My wife Lucienne and I were visiting with Clarence at his home in Beaverton, near Portland, when Clarence suggested that we take a trip to Buell. We thought this was a splendid idea, and the next morning Clarence, his daughter Claire Walker Tri, Lucienne and I were on our way to Sheridan. From there, it took us ten minutes to drive to Buell—a trip that had taken three hours in our time.

On our way we passed a field where a man was operating a combine. It struck me that that one man with his machine replaced a crew of 25 men, a cook and waitress, 18 horses, a huge steam engine, a grain separator fifty feet long, and eight wagons. It was a symbol of how life had changed in the years since we left Buell.

When we reached Buell, the changes were more than we had imagined. We had a hard time getting oriented. The store, house, orchard, barn, fences, even the small square building with the crescent in the door, all were gone. The blacksmith shop was gone, and so were the scales, the Woodman of the World Lodge, and our grammar school. The well where we had drawn water with a bucket and stored butter in summer was filled in. The gardens, pastures and fields were added to an adjoining farm.

There was a convenience store across the road from where our store had been, but that was about all Buell offered. The Methodist church was closed, boarded up. The public campground was now a State Park with barbeque facilities, and there was a new school—the children were bussed.

The improved roads had been the country store's Waterloo. As it became easy for people to travel back and forth to the larger towns, the country store was no longer the vital supply point it had been during our time.

Clarence and I went to see the old swimming hole where we had learned to swim in our birthday suits. The water was nearly gone because the timber at the headwaters of Mill Creek had been cut down and forests no longer held back the winter rains.

We returned to the place where the country store had been. Nearby stood a large maple tree—it was one that Clarence and I had dug from the woods as a small sapling seventy-five years before, and planted near the path from the store to the house. The maple tree was all that remained of all our time at Buell.

Standing there in silence with Clarence, my mind went back to the days when Buell was the center of life for several communities. It was here our parents worked, struggled from a humble beginning and built a successful business, which they sacrificed to give their sons a better education. Here Clarence and I played and worked, and spent a slice of our formative years together. Everything was changed and gone, including our parents and all the friends and people who had come to the country store. It was a nostalgic moment, and an axiom came to mind—nothing in this life is permanent except change.

As we walked back to our car, Clarence remarked, "George, the time we spent here was Buell's finest hour."

George F. Walker

My Dynamo Husband

By Lucienne C. Walker

George and I met in July, 1943, in Sacramento, California at the Navy Recruiting Station. He was assigned to Sacramento WAVES Recruitment Program and I was a WAVE Recruiter assigned to the Office of Naval Officer Procurement in San Francisco.

Before leaving for my Sacramento assignment, my commanding officer told me that the two previous WAVES assigned to Sacramento found George F. Walker uncooperative, and hoped things would be better for me. I must admit I was a bit nervous about the assignment, but it was a challenge and I was determined to make good.

Moments after reporting to the Navy officer at the Recruiting Station, I was face to face with this supposedly difficult man. The officer introduced us, we greeted each other and shook hands. George was cold and aloof, eyeing me with steely eyes. I, too, eyed him. He didn't know I was aware of his lack of cooperation with the two previous WAVES. I knew I had to say something to reach him. With my best smile I said, "Mr. Walker, I'm delighted to be here and am anxious to work with you to make the WAVES program a success."

He smiled and commented, "This, I'll appreciate."

It broke the ice and from that moment on we worked extremely well together. He was a very conscientious, hard working man and expected me to carry my share of the work which I was happy to do. Soon Sacramento had the most successful WAVES program in the entire 12th Naval District.

I soon learned why the two previous WAVES had not succeeded with George. The first wanted to run the program, give orders, and not do any work; the second was unsuited for the job. So his skepticism was justifiable when he met me.

George was forty-five when I met him. Had he delayed enlisting in the Navy by four days, he would have been exempt from the service, since the upper age limit for draftees was lowered.

When George's wife heard that I had to eat all my meals in restaurants, she kindly invited me to a delicious home cooked dinner. We became friends and kept in touch throughout the years with the exchange of Christmas cards and infrequent letters. After the war, George returned to his position at Standard Oil and was soon transferred to New York, while I went back to my native New Hampshire.

It was nearly twenty years before I saw George again. In 1963 he was retired and a widower of three years. He eased into his retirement by traveling all around the world. On his way back home to California after his trip, he stopped in New York, and we had dinner and a brief visit. I hadn't seen George since 1944.

When we met we were both surprised at one another's changed physical appearance. We were both gray with a few wrinkles, but still slender and sturdy. The one thing that hadn't changed was our friendship.

This was the beginning of a steady stream of letters crossing the continent back and forth, telephone calls, and several air trips. After a year of this long distance courtship we were married in 1965 and settled in Walnut Creek, California.

I have often wondered if destiny played a part in my being assigned to the Office of Naval Officer Procurement in San Francisco, when I could have been assigned anywhere in the United States, and if it was destiny when George enlisted in the Navy four days too soon.

In marriage we soon got to know each other better. We learned about our childhoods, schooling, goals, careers, likes, dislikes, and philosophy in general.

I learned that after George's Army discharge at the end of World War I, he enrolled at the University of Oregon. He financed three semesters of college working at various jobs—peeling potatoes and waiting on tables in the dining room, selling a photographer's pictures at fraternity dances, and working as the agent for a laundry firm in Eugene. In the summer he worked with pick and shovel on country roads, and worked in a sawmill.

On the way home to see his father at Christmas vacation, while waiting for the bus in the lobby of the Bligh Hotel in Salem, George met a representative of a newly published magazine, *The Northwest Warriors*. He was looking for men to sell subscriptions and suggested George give it a try in a nearby office building while waiting for the bus.

George sold four subscriptions in a half hour. Two days later George was on his way to take the agency in Nebraska and Iowa, trip paid, and a supply of subscription receipts for collections payable to the solicitor.

When he arrived in Omaha, George got the surprise of his life—the temperature averaged twenty degrees below zero, with two feet of snow on the ground. He managed to peddle enough magazines to stay alive until March.

When growing up on the farm, George developed a closeness and love for land and always wanted to own land. While selling subscriptions he learned homestead land was available, and set out to find some. In a homestead deal, the government bet the homesteader it could starve him out in less than three years. But George, with Clarence's help, held out and acquired homestead land a few miles outside Casa Grande, Arizona, which they held for 52 years.

In 1922 George returned to Portland, went to work on a service station for Standard Oil Company of California, the beginning of a 41-year career. From this humble beginning he climbed numerous rungs up the ladder, traveling extensively in the fifty states, either for the company or on his own.

It was during our quiet discussions I discovered George had a unique and interesting story to tell. His personal experiences were history in the making. I urged and encouraged him to write his Oregon childhood experiences.

Perhaps due to his childhood training, George developed a tremendous drive, and whatever he starts he tackles with enthusiasm and tenacity. He's a self-starter and a doer. If a job needs to be done he does it.

George's dry wit and humorous side help release the stress of daily living. He never fails to pull one on me to bring a laugh.

Still feeling the love of land, most of his retirement time is spent planting and attending a large vegetable and fruit garden on our terraced hillside. He has a large patch of a variety of berries, a small orchard of fruit trees, and several kinds of grapes, which keep us both busy canning, freezing and jamming. At fall time the freezer and larder are full of the summer harvest, ready to enjoy in the winter months.

From a sod house on the Kansas prairie, and four score and four years later, George, a graduate of the "University of Hard Knocks," adds another experience, that of authorship, to his life's work and accomplishments.